Rescued for a Second Chance

Jewells Jewells

ISBN: Ebook 979-8-9952772-0-0
ISBN: Paperback 979-8-9952772-1-7
ISBN: Hardcover 979-8-9952772-2-4

Acknowledgements

First and foremost, I thank Jesus for rescuing me and giving me a second chance at life.

To my editor, Rosalie, thank you for helping bring this testimony to life and for your patience as we worked through every detail of this journey.

Jeanine, Sonja, and Anna, your love and friendship mean everything to me. Thank you for being part of my story and for walking this journey with me.

To my friends who have supported me privately throughout this process—you know who you are— thank you for listening, believing, and encouraging me to share what God has done.

I'm deeply grateful to the congregation at the Mission church in Vacaville, whose prayers, encouragement, and support have been instrumental in my spiritual healing and growth.

To Sacramento Christian Healing Ministries (SCHM), thank you for providing the healing class

that became a catalyst for my healing. Your ministry
created the space where God could begin restoring
what had been lost.

Table of Contents

PART I

BEFORE THE CRASH

Chapter One:

Ordinary Day, Extraordinary Fate

The last thing I remember before the collision was having a brief conversation with my mother. Seconds later, another car was heading right for us. The unthinkable occurred, the car hit us head on.

The disbelief set in fast. Was this really happening? Everything felt like it was in slow motion physically but my mind was thinking quick. Even at twelve-years-old I knew this was not going to turn out good.

December 18, 1987 was the night everything changed. To really understand what took place, let me take you back to why we were on that road.

Grass Valley, California was about an hour drive from where I lived in Sacramento, California. Every year in December that town would close off the main street and do a festival called Cornish Christmas. We would finish out the Friday school day and run home in anticipation for the night to come. It was a time of fun for my family and a start to the Christmas and New Year's holiday break from school. This was the family tradition for as long as I could remember.

The first thing we did when we got to the Cornish Christmas festival was have dinner. We would go to the same place every year—a little shop that served a food item that the California gold miners used to eat decades ago called a pasty. It's like a meat pie folded into a half-moon shape. We always ate our pasty's before walking the Main Street to see everything. The warm, flaky crust and savory filling were perfect on a cold December night.

Once everyone finished eating, we walked the street looking in the shops. Food vendors lined the sidewalks on both sides. Eventually we would stop for the annual hot chocolate to warm our hands.

There was always a Santa Claus somewhere along Main Street. Even though my mom had told us she bought our Christmas presents—no need to pretend otherwise—we still got to have fun sitting on Santa's lap and telling him what we wanted for Christmas. I would usually make up something on the spot since my mom was standing right there listening, and I did not want to tell Santa what I really wanted with her hearing every word. This and so much more was all part of what made this annual night so special for me.

Let me take you back a few years before 1987 to 1984 when I was 9 years old. My family started to attend a new church that had younger families. There were about five or six families at this church that began to create a community together. This is how I met my friend Jill who was also 9 years old. Jill was in the car crash with me.

The first time Jill and I met was at a Chuck E. Cheese's Pizza restaurant. Our families had gone together after church one Sunday. My mom told me beforehand that I would be meeting Jill and that maybe we could become friends.

Upon arriving at the restaurant, we met Jill's mom and dad. Jill's mom told me Jill was probably at the skee-ball machines and gave me a description of what she looked like. I was off to find her, my potential new friend.

I walked up to the girl who was at the skee-ball machine and asked, "Are you Jill?"

She said yes and asked if I wanted to play skee-ball with her.

We spent the next few hours playing games, comparing tickets, and laughing at the animatronic band. By the time our parents said it was time to leave, we had already made plans to sit together in Sunday school the next week. Some friendships take time to build. Ours started instantly.

Our small group of friends from church did many things together. We had summer barbecues and swim parties. We also celebrated everyone's birthdays. Best of all, our New Year's Eve parties were legendary. We would take over someone's house—the kids would run wild while the adults talked. We stayed up with anticipation until midnight, and when the clock struck twelve, everyone went outside with noisemakers and pots to bang and ring in the new year. We felt so grown up, being allowed to stay awake that late. Through all of these memorable events we became very close, even like a close-knit family.

Though this was a church group, the existence of a god never crossed my mind. I would not say I was an atheist. Having or not having a belief in God was just not important to me. I was living my life. Thoughts about death or the meaning of life or even what would happen to me if I passed away were not things I thought about. Most children would not be thinking of such things. We went to church and to school because we had to, nothing more.

Time passed and our group started to show interest in my family's tradition of going to Grass Valley's Cornish Christmas. The decision was made the

Christmas of 1987. We would all go as a caravan and enjoy the festival together. It was exciting to include my friends (my chosen family) along with my actual family. Everyone was excited.

The very last road you drive on to get to Grass Valley from Sacramento is a highway called Highway 49. It is a road named for the gold mining gold rush of 1849 and connects the towns, north to south, along the western side of the Sierra Mountain range. In 1987 this section of road was winding with a single lane going each direction.

The collision took place just south from Grass Valley in an area called Alta Sierra. This particular location on Highway 49 is known to be a very dangerous road with a history of head-on collisions. That rainy December night we were not thinking about the dangers. We were thinking about the pasty's, the hot chocolates, the shopping and Santa Claus.

That day began as normal as a day ever could. I went to school knowing that when class was out for the day it would be two whole weeks before I would have to return to school. It was exciting to have such a break. In addition, we would be going to the Christmas festival along with our friends. This made the day even more special.

After lunch at school, something began to change where suddenly I no longer wanted to go to the festival in Grass Valley. I did not know what it was, the excited feeling was no longer present. Instead, I had a feeling of dread as if knowing something bad was going to happen.

When I got home from school that day, I found my mom in the kitchen. "Mom, I don't want to go tonight". She looked up from what she was doing, saying: "What? Why not? You love Cornish Christmas."

That was true, I really did love Cornish Christmas, but the feeling of dread was still there.

"I don't know," I told her. "I just have this bad feeling."

She paused, studying my face. "That's strange," she said quietly. "I've been feeling the same way all day." We stood there a moment longer. Neither of us knew what to make of it.

Once everyone showed up to our house and we loaded up in cars, the feeling of dread and not wanting to go left. Now we were on the road to Cornish Christmas.

Chapter Two:

The Caravan Rule

We had one simple rule for our group when doing events that required a caravan; you go home in the same car you came in, sometimes in the same seat. Going to the Christmas festival that night, I rode in our friend Allen's station wagon. I sat in the very back seat with another child from our group.

Rules can become bent in ways that change everything. That night would prove to be one of those nights.

We arrived at the festival in what felt like half the time. We went right away to get our pasty's. We were kind of a large group so the adults decided we should spilt up into smaller groups and meet up at the hot chocolate stand later. We walked the streets and had fun window shopping. We met up around 8:30pm at the hot chocolate stand and had our hot drinks.

A little after 9pm, we all decided to head back home. We were all walking to the cars after we were done at the festival when I noticed my little sister walking with us to Allen's station wagon. I told her that this was the wrong car but she ignored me.

When the station wagon doors opened, my little sister planted herself in the backseat and crossed her arms. I looked at her with a look that stated I wanted her to follow the rules.

"Get out and go back to the car you came here in."

"I'm not getting out," she announced, "you can ride in the other car." I argued with her and stated that this is not the rule. She just sat there and put her head down and would not acknowledge me any further.

I looked at Allen for direction. I asked, "what do I do? She won't move." He looked around and saw the car she had traveled in, so he pointed in that direction and told me to hurry and just switch places. I went to the other car but I was mad about it. Allen probably just wanted a quick solution so we could get on the road.

The other car was my family's Chevy Blazer. I climbed into the very back of the Blazer, still angry. There was no seat back there, just floor space and most of that was taken up by Allen's baby's stroller. I wedged myself in next to it, trying to find a comfortable position. There wasn't one.

My dad was driving my family's Chevy Blazer. Jill's dad sat in the front passenger seat. In the middle there were three seats, a bench style seat. My mom was behind the driver, my friend Jill was in the middle and her mom was in the remaining seat on the passenger side. We headed out for home on Highway 49 with our family's Chevy Blazer being the last to leave in the caravan.

Despite my irritation about the seating situation, the mood in the car was good. Mom and Jill's mom were talking about maybe doing this every year as a tradition.

From my cramped spot in the back, I could see out the rear window into the darkness. The road behind us was mostly empty—just one car a little way back. As we weaved with the windy mountain road, the headlights behind us would disappear and reappear. The others from our group were somewhere up ahead. We were pretty much alone on that dark road heading back home.

I shifted, trying to get comfortable, knocking my legs up against the stroller.

"You doing okay back there?" Mom asked, turning slightly.

"Yeah, I'm fine", even though I really was not but we would be home soon enough.

Chapter Three:

Collision Course

It was cold in the back—colder than it was up front by the heater. I pulled my jacket tighter and tried to settle in for the drive home. December nights in these mountains get frigid. In the small amount of light coming in the car, I could see my breath.

Somewhere down the road, a woman was just about to leave her granddaughters home for a short drive to her own home. She told her family she was not feeling well. The family tried to get her to stay the night as it was already after 9pm but she insisted she was good enough to drive home. She got in her car and headed on to Highway 49 in the direction of Grass Valley.

No one could have known that the combination of decisions would accumulate into one very horrific collision. My sister's stubbornness to follow the rules delayed our departure. The woman's family delayed her departure by holding her back with her not realizing she was having a medical emergency. The two cars were now in sync for a collision.

There are small ups and downs in life but then there are things that change your life forever. This was our moment in time, a pivot point in our lives.

We had not been on Highway 49 very long when Dad's voice changed. "What is this car doing?"

His tone made everyone stop talking. I leaned to the side trying to see better through the front windshield.

Up ahead, headlights were swerving back and forth across the road—first in their lane, then crossing into ours, then back again into their lane. The car looked out of control. That car had to be out of control! Something was wrong with that driver!

Our cars kept getting closer and closer. Those headlights kept swerving—left, right, left. Why wouldn't that car stay in their lane? Why wouldn't my dad slow down?

The headlights swerved into our lane again, but this time they stayed there. Those headlights were coming right at us! They were growing brighter with every second. Then we were so close that I could see the headlights aiming directly at me. It was all happening so fast but felt like it took forever.

From the front passenger's seat, my friend's dad yelled "look out!" and tried to grab the steering wheel from my dad but it was too late. That car hit us straight on. I will never forget the loud booming sound that came at impact.

As soon as the car hit us, it crushed the hood of our car so we could no longer see out the front windshield. It was like slow motion. I remember the feeling of disbelief as it was happening. Strange things go through your mind during traumatic events. The others in the car may have had other thoughts but my thought was just simple, 'this is really bad'.

This slow-motion feel kept going. I noticed I was floating up off the floor of the car towards the ceiling. Those in the middle seat were also floating. I was just touching the ceiling when I could feel an intense amount of energy from the impact. It felt as if it went all over the car.

Then, suddenly, everything changed.

It was as if something had picked up the rear passenger side of the car and flipped the car up into the air, flipped three times from front to back while spinning around like an arrow.

I could not understand what was happening. I think I hit my head on the ceiling. I was dizzy and everything looked dark. Someone was screaming and everyone was falling on top of each other. Only the two in the front had their seat belts fastened.

Those of us without seat belts were being violently thrown around. At one point I hit something or landed on something in the car that knocked the air out of me. Then it felt as if everyone fell on me. I remember saying I can't breathe while gasping for air. Again, we were tossed around and I found myself on my back with everyone under my legs. Somehow, as a twelve-year-old, this was the moment I knew that I was in danger of dying.

The car was turning in a direction that made everyone slide my way and under me. Somehow I knew that their weight put me in danger. The car's flipping and spinning had forced them under my legs with their momentum pushing up against my body. The back of my shoulders was against the car as I felt their increasing weight beginning to crush me. Somehow I moved my legs off of them. I had the thought that I had successfully moved but the car turned again shifting us so they were all under my legs again. It turned out that my successful move would not be the case. I felt my chin coming close to my chest and I somehow knew this was going to be the end. I heard and felt a cracking inside my neck. I saw flashes of light inside of my head. My throat began filling with a fluid. I felt myself sigh and give up. I fell out of my body and on to the road.

PART II

DEATH AND THE OTHER SIDE

Chapter Four:

The Moment Between Worlds

There I was standing on the asphalt highway, looking up at the car as it completed its final rollover. The car flew past me and landed upside down about 30 feet away. It hit the ground so hard there was a rumble that appeared to come towards me and go under my feet. The car skidded on the road creating sparks that looked like a fourth of July firework.

My first thought, as the car finally stopped resting on the guardrail and everything grew quiet was, "how did I get out of the car?" For a very brief moment, I had not realized that I was dead. Somehow, I forgot what had just happened to me. I just knew that I was now out of the car.

I tried to understand what had happened. One second, I was being crushed, unable to breathe, my neck making cracking sounds and the next second I was... here. Standing. Breathing—or was I breathing?

It was as if someone grabbed me from the inside and yelled "look!". I stared down the road at the car and then I saw it through the car window. My body laying lifeless in the car. Even from where I stood on the road, I could see my body was not moving. No rise and fall of breathing. No twitching or shifting. Just… still. I wanted to look away but could not. That was me in there! My body! But I was also here, standing on the road, looking at it. How could I be in two places at the same time?

First, I looked down at my hands. Then I looked at the rest of me. I looked like a ghost wearing ghostly clothes that looked like the sweat suit outfit and jacket I was wearing that night. The disconnect felt impossible. Like trying to hold two opposite thoughts in my mind at the same time. I am dead. I am alive. I am in the car. I am on the road. Both were true. Both were impossible.

Suddenly I noticed there was a strange darkness slowly coming towards me from all directions. It looked like a black fog. This darkness was coming towards me from all around and it also felt like there were eyes everywhere watching me. I felt scared and cold. Then, after a few seconds, the darkness was gone. Slowly everything appeared to lose temperature as if the existence of temperature was gone. I could no longer feel the air around me. It should have been cold in the mountains in December but I was not cold. It was not warm. It was not hot. It was nothing. How do you explain that?

Down the road, in the opposite direction of our car, I could see the woman's car that hit us along with a pickup truck next to it. The truck had been following behind her car that was going towards Grass Valley. The truck was not able to stop. The truck hit the back driver's side of the woman's car after she had crashed into us. That pick-up truck stopped her car from continuing to spin around.

While looking at the car and the truck, the woman came out of her car but she was dead. Unlike me, she did not look like a ghost. She appeared to have a more solid shape that glowed a golden color.

As I watched the woman standing by her car, a man suddenly appeared standing next to her. They were talking and staring over at me. I wanted to know what they were talking about. I thought to myself, I need to get closer. Suddenly, I was right next to them! How did I do that?

I tried to listen but it was as if I could not hear them. How could this be as I was standing right next to them? On top of this, it was as if they were ignoring me.

Frustrated, I decided I would just go back to where I was first standing on the road. One thought is all it took and I was there instantly.

I looked back at the woman's car. Now there were two more beings standing there with them. These two new beings were shaped like people but they were a solid golden light. Today, I think of them as glowing lightbulb people. They reminded me of the aliens in the 1980s movie Cocoon. The woman looked at me and waved. Then the two lightbulb beings, one on each side of her, took her by the arms and shot up into the sky. They moved so fast they all looked like a comet. They were heading for a bright light way up in the sky. Once they reached that light they were gone and so was that light in the sky. I looked back towards her car where they had been standing to see what that man was doing.

He was gone.

Somehow in that moment I knew I could not go where that woman went. There appeared to be some rule that did not allow me to go there. I decided I could get answers from the others in my car once they also died. I waited and looked. At some point, a sudden realization hit me.

None of the rest of those in the car with me had died. It was only me.

Never had I felt so alone as I did in that moment. I started to panic. There must be someone who could help me. I began to yell out. Help! Help! Someone, help me! There was no one. I yelled even louder.

At the back window of the car appeared my friend Jill. She was hitting the window with her fist and yelling for help. She suddenly stopped and looked at me with a questioning look at what she could be seeing in the dark. Her expression changed as she realized it was me. She went away from the window, crawling back to where my body was laying. I watched as she checked for my heartbeat and for my breath.

Jill then hurried back to the window and called out my name. I asked her if she could see me. She nodded her head yes. I was surprised. She then asked me to come to the window. I thought ok and suddenly I was right in front of her at the window. I did not walk to the window; I was just there.

She asked, "how did you do that?" I told her, "I do not know. I just thought to come over to you and I was here."

She asked "are you dead?" I nodded my head yes. She asked "does it hurt to be dead?". I said "no."

She said "can you get back in your body?" I told her, "I cannot even get back into the car so how am I going to get in my body?"

She said "just try." So, I tried to get back into the car. Nothing I tried would work.

Suddenly Jill started to call my name and ask where I went. I then realized that she could not see me anymore. I watched her check my body again. She was crying now as if I was gone, as if I was gone for good. I wanted so much to be alive again.

Chapter Five:

Bargains and Promises

As I stood by the car trying to figure out how to get back in my body, the man who had been with the woman in the other car was now standing next to me. There were also two other beings standing there as well. These were different from the lightbulb people. These beings reminded me of Ogres. Not like the cute green one from the Shrek movie. These were dark greyish in color and tall with scary looking faces and lots of teeth. Some of their teeth stuck out of their mouths like a bulldog's teeth. The kind of sharp pointy teeth that stick up from the bottom jaw.

They appeared to be waiting for something.

They were waiting for me!

A feeling of dread came over me. The man said I had to go with these creatures. I did NOT want to go with them, anywhere. I asked the man if I could stay with him. He said it was the rules that I would have to go with them. I protested. The man told the ogre like creatures to hold on a moment while he talked to me. He took me aside as if he did not want the creatures to hear what he was going to tell me. He told me to trust him and that he needed my help. He needed me to help a friend of his named Fernando. He did not want the creatures to know what he was doing.

Looking over the man's shoulder, I glanced at the creatures waiting nearby. They looked impatient, hungry even. "But where are they taking me?", I asked.

"I can't explain everything right now," he said quietly. "But I promise I'll come for you. I won't leave you there. Just trust me. Can you do that?"

There was something about the man's face and his voice that made me want to trust him. Even though nothing made sense, even though I was terrified, I heard myself say, "Okay. I'll help."

I was very scared. What was I agreeing to anyway? Where were they going to take me? What were they planning to do to me?

The man told me to stand by the car with my hands up on the car. It was like what police officers tell people to do when they are about to be arrested. He said to just stand there. I stood there crying, feeling the panic grow inside.

After what felt like just a few moments, one of the creatures grabbed me and lifted me over his shoulder so I was looking behind it. The creature began to run away from the car into the forest. As the creature ran, I could see my friend Jill still in the car. That mystery man was suddenly gone. Just gone—again.

Through the trees, I could still barely make out the lights from the crash scene, Jill's face still in the window. Then the darkness swallowed everything. The darkness closed in until I could no longer see the car or my friend. I could only see the forest of trees.

The forest rushed past in a blur. I could feel the rhythm of the creature's running—impossibly fast, inhuman. The December cold that should have been freezing felt like nothing against my ghostly body.

There were only the two creatures, the forest, me, and the unknown ahead of us. My thought at that moment was, 'what had I been thinking to agree to this?' I could not help but think I had made a big mistake.

Chapter Six

Descent into Darkness

As the ogre-like creature carried me deeper into darkness, one thought kept haunting me: What if that mystery man does not keep his promise? What if he does not come for me? I wondered if I would be able to find this person named Fernando.

We appeared to move really fast in what I can only guess was an easterly direction. We could have gone as far as the middle of America but I am just not sure. Finally, we stopped. The creature set me down. We were surrounded by darkness. The only light I could see was the dim white glow of my ghostly body.

There was another, a third one of these creatures standing in some strange box. Suddenly I realized it was some kind of elevator. The creature that had carried me told me to get in the elevator. The creature in the elevator asked who I was and where was the person they were supposed to bring. The two creatures just said "we could not get that one so we brought her." The one in the elevator said "the boss is going to be angry." I wondered who they were talking about. Who were they supposed to bring and who is this boss?

The three creatures and I got in the elevator. The elevator started to move, seemingly down as if it was going into the earth. We were moving fast but I could still make out what looked like rock walls, as if we were in a vertical tunnel. Wind whistled past as we plummeted deeper and deeper. How far down were we going? With every second of descent, the dread in my chest grew heavier. We were all quiet and after a little bit, the elevator stopped. The two original creatures and I got out. The third creature stayed in the elevator.

We began to walk forward through rock canyon walls on both sides and above. We walked about sixty feet when the wall on the left side ended and we were coming into an open space.

When the wall on the left ended, I saw it. A massive round pit, maybe forty feet deep with a diameter of around thirty feet. Fire blazed at the bottom—not normal fire, but something angrier.

At the top of the fiery pit stood a black creature with wings. As I watched, it grabbed a ghostly looking person from a platform and shoved her over the edge into the fire that was at the bottom. I gasped inside as the ghostly body hit the fire and instantly became a skeleton. Then the skeleton swam—actually swam—through the flames to reach a ladder. She climbed out, and as she emerged from the deep pit, she transformed back into a ghostly form.

There was a line. A long line of ghostly souls waiting their turn and I realized with horror: this was not a one-time punishment. This was happening over and over and over again. The ghostly souls would climb out, get back in line, and eventually be thrown in again. How long had they been doing this? How long would it continue?

Turning my attention back to the direction we were walking in, I could feel my heart fill with hopelessness. I had never felt hopeless like this before. It was a deep and crippling experience.

I did not want to watch people being pushed into the pit of fire any longer. I did not want to be there anymore. How would I ever get out? With every amount of energy I had, I ran. Back towards the elevator I went without really thinking of what I would do next. The third ogre creature was still in the elevator. The two ogre creatures caught up to me and grabbed me. They told me not to try it again, then they made me walk back with them. I realized then, there was no way out.

The two creatures were walking just a little ahead of me, one on either side. The one on the right started looking back at me. Staring at his face I noticed he appeared to want to communicate something to me. I focused more on his facial expression. He gave the impression to be sympathetic to my situation. I felt my emotions lightening up. Perhaps I have a friend here.

No!

As soon as I connected with this creature he began to laugh. He said to the other creature, "oh look, she thinks we care. Ha, ha, ha."

At the realization that the creature had tricked me, I began to feel a very strong rage welling up in me. Without thinking, I jumped on the creature's back and started punching him in the back of the head. Over and over, I hit that creature as hard as I could because that creature had just tricked me and laughed at me. A left and a right and another left until the other creature grabbed me and threw me to the dirty ground. They both started punching and kicking me. As I was on the ground, I thought to myself "why are they doing this. It's not like they can kill me, I am already dead". After a few seconds of them beating on me, they picked me up off the ground and we proceeded to walk forward. I could not imagine what I would experience next.

Chapter Seven

The Wrong Soul?

The rage inside me had not settled as we walked forward. I was still replaying what had just happened-the trick, the beating, being thrown to the ground like I was nothing. I wanted to fight back but knew it would get me nowhere. These creatures were in control, and I was completely at their mercy — with no idea where they were taking me. Nothing about this place had been good so far, and deep down, I already knew — it wasn't going to be.

As we walked forward, out in front of us I could see something that resembled a lake. The lake was not water but fire that appeared to have no source as to why it was burning. This fire lake also appeared to be floating. I could see tunnels below or underneath this fire lake. Lava was coming in waves that flowed one direction through the tunnels under this fire lake. There were ghostly souls down inside the tunnels. They were chained to the walls of the tunnels. The lava went over them and they let out screams and cries.

To my right along the side of the lake was a rock cliff. Ghostly souls were also chained to the side of the cliff. The fire was flowing like water to reach up the rocks and splash over the people chained to the rocks. These chained ghostly souls were also all crying and screaming.

Suddenly over this lake appeared a winged creature that was all black. Reminded me of what people consider as angels but somehow not a nice angel. It flew over the fire and just as fast as it had appeared it also disappeared.

Then came another creature, different from all the rest of the creatures I had seen up to this point. This one headed towards where we were standing on the dirt path. The ogre like creatures that were taking me along this dirt path were maybe six to seven feet tall. This new creature towered over them maybe as much as being four feet taller. It had two feet that were like goat hooves and horns on its head like a spiral-horned antelope. These two spiral horns were about four feet long. This strange looking creature came very close to me. It bent over towards me; its black stone eyes got directly in my face. It was mesmerizing. It felt as if it was searching my soul. Suddenly it backed up in fierce anger. In a loud voice it stated, "you brought me the daughter, I wanted the mother." The two ogre creatures started to explain why they brought me instead. I figured this was the boss the creature in the elevator had mentioned. Why did this thing want my mom?

The ogre creatures explained how I was the only one that died and that someone named Jesus had shown up. I was the only one they could bring down there. Was the mystery man who they were talking about, the one they were calling Jesus? The man who secretly told me he would come for me? That must be who they were talking about because there wasn't anyone else at the crash.

The angry creature then said, "she is too pure, we can't even torture her. Go put her next to that guy Fernando". Wait, did he just say Fernando. Maybe I would find him after all. The ogre creature said "ok boss", then the very tall creature disappeared.

So that is the boss.

The three of us walked to the edge of the fire lake. A metal disc like object about twenty feet in diameter, was coming over the lake towards us. It stopped at the edge. We stepped on to the disc. It began to move up and forward. It moved over the fire lake, which I now realized was a winding river of fire.

Along this fire river, there was a rock cliff on the right of us. On the left was a row of high-rise buildings that seem to be five or six floors that were visible. The buildings stretched upwards, but I was not able to see beyond the fifth or sixth floor as there was a rock ceiling above that cut off the visibility of the other floors.

We made a turn to the left. From there, the fire river wound on for miles. Still there was the cliff to the right and buildings to left. All along the way I could see people chained to the cliff.

At some point, the disc stopped on the edge by the buildings. We got off and started to walk to the doors of one of the buildings.

From the outside I could see into the building. Each floor had rooms. Ghostly souls were being tortured in these rooms. I could see a room on the first floor that had someone strapped down on a hospital style bed. There was ogre like creatures torturing the ghostly person. They moved a little and I could see the person's face. I recognized the person from pictures in my school books. This was Hitler. He looked at me. I can see and feel the regret in his eyes.

We entered the building through a doorway and walked up to an elevator. We got into the elevator and started going up. Each floor I could see more high-ranking Nazi's in rooms being tortured. I also saw European Royals and Napoleon. There were many others but I did not recognize them. There were also many rooms that were empty.

As we went up into the higher floors, the river of fire was no longer visible and the degree of torturing was lessening. It was now so dark without the glow of the fire. I could only see the dim light coming from the ghostly souls. I lost count of how many floors but it was a lot. Maybe as many as 100 floors or more.

We finally stopped. It felt like we were at the top floor. The rooms were now small cells about five-foot square with transparent walls. Only room enough to sit or stand but not lay down. It was a very confined space.

We stepped out of the elevator and started walking down a hall. There are cells on both sides with people inside. As we got close to the cell, they were going to place me, one man in a cell started yelling. "Let me out. Let me out". He yelled these words over and over. He was losing control so the creature's started beating him. I felt so angry that I jumped on the back of one of them and started hitting it in the back of its head. They threw me to the ground in a cell and started kicking me and hitting me. Even though I was already dead, I could feel every impact. Not physical pain exactly, but something different. It was as if it shut down my mind.

I curled up, trying to protect myself, knowing it was pointless. When they finally stopped, I felt something I had never experienced before: complete powerlessness. I could not believe they did this again. They could do this whenever they wanted. For however long I was here.

Sitting on that cell floor, I had never felt more hopeless. How would I ever get out of this place? The man in the cell next to me started to talk to me. He was saying hello in a very quiet voice. I found it very hard to stop crying but I finally stopped long enough to say hello. He answered, "hello, my name is Fernando".

Chapter Eight

Love's Sacrifice, Heaven's Answer

In all the darkness and horror, I had witnessed so far, nothing had prepared me for the simple relief of hearing a gentle voice say, "hello, my name is Fernando". I stopped crying and looked up at the man who was talking to me from the other side of a transparent wall. This was Fernando that the mystery man had told me to help. What was I going to do to help him? I was also a prisoner of this awful place. There was no way we would be able to get out the way I got there. I had already tried once and failed.

Fernando was talking with me but why was he trying to be so quiet? I asked in a very normal voice, "why are you talking so quietly?" Everyone that was close by shushed me. Then I heard it and knew why. Another ogre creature said in the deepest most echoing voice, "be quiet."

Fernando spoke in a whisper, "they don't like for us to make any noise but if we talk quietly, they don't seem to hear us." I could tell he had an accent so I asked him where he was from. He said he was from Argentina. He then asked me where I was from and I told him America. Others nearby heard me say America and started to ask where is this America. I answered, "how do you not know?" Fernando told them it was a newer country like his.

The ogre creatures spoke again, "be quiet".

We had to stop talking for a little while and I took the opportunity to look around. I could see ghostly souls everywhere. You could hear these ogre creatures saying be quiet all over but I was not able to see them. This place was so dark. There must be a lot of them I thought.

Suddenly there was one walking past me in what appeared to be a hall. I was only able to see the creature because of the glow of my ghostly looking body shining on him. The man that had been getting beaten when I got there turned my direction after the creature passed by him. He said "for what it's worth, thank you for trying to help." I understood him as there was no real way to help or to be helped here.

Back to talking with Fernando, he began to ask if I knew him. I said, "how would I know you, I just got here?" He asked me, "do you know about me back in the other life?" I said "no" and asked "why, who are you?" He started to explain that he was Fernando Paternoster from the Olympic football team that won the silver medal for Argentina. Realizing I had told him I was American, he said, "In your country they call it soccer". I told him I was not interested in sports so I would not really know about him.

Fernando changed the subject and asked how old I was and I told him twelve. This appeared to worry him. He started to question why I was there. He stated that I was so young. Looking around I realized that everyone was very old. I had not seen any children, so I asked if there were any young people there. There was a girl that was 16 and a boy 17 nearby but everyone else was older, all of them were adults.

I asked Fernando what happened to him. He stated he passed away on June 6, 1967, just after he turned 64. It was something with his heart but he was not quite sure what happened. It was as if he could not remember. I asked how he ended up here because he gave the impression of being a nice man. He said he was a very nice person in life and just never got born again. I had heard of born again from going to church. I thought maybe that is why I am here too.

His death in 1967 got me thinking—what about the others? I looked around and asked what about these others? Fernando began to tell me the years each one had arrived there. One was there from the 1340's. Another didn't speak a language that anyone knew but he was dressed in clothes that made me think he looked like he was from the Christopher Columbus era. Then I asked who had been there the longest.

There was a strange silence. Everyone in the rows of cells in front of me moved just a little to the left. There was a cell about 5 rows up. In it sat a man on the ground not moving. He did not talk or even turn his head at all. Fernando said he had guessed this man was there since around 340 A.D. but no one knew for certain as this man never spoke to any of them.

The atmosphere around me began to shift and I recognized that all eyes were on me. The others were telling Fernando to ask me. I responded, "ask me what?" Fernando began to explain how he was the last one to arrive in that area so they were wondering what year I died. They all stared at me waiting for me to reply. In my head I was thinking this is not going to go over well. How could they not know what year it is? Unsure this was the best thing for me to do, I reluctantly stated "it's 1987".

Everyone gasped. The sound echoed through the cells— dozens of souls inhaling in shock at the same moment.

"Nineteen eighty-seven," Fernando kept repeating. "Nineteen eighty-seven. That can't be right. That means…" His voice trailed off as the math hit him. "Twenty years. I've been here twenty years?" He said "how can it be 1987? What about my family and friends? How can I tell them not to come here?"

Other voices started murmuring, calculating their own time lost. Someone started crying. Everyone was getting really upset. The noise level was increasing. They were getting louder. Chaos was spreading. I had just destroyed whatever fragile hope these souls had been clinging to. Time meant nothing here—they could be here for decades and never know it.

I asked Fernando, "How is it you don't know the year?"

"There is no way of telling how long you have been here," he said.

"But you've been here twenty years. How long do you think I've been here?", I asked.

"I don't know. I don't know.", Fernando exclaimed.

"Guess," I pressed him.

He was quiet for a moment. "If I had to guess… maybe five years."

Five years. The words hit me like a blow. I would never leave this place if it was already five years.

A couple of the ogre creatures came. They were demanding for everyone to be quiet. Then this really grumpy guy a couple rows ahead turned and pointed at me and said "it's all her fault!"

Now the creatures were heading straight for my cell, their intentions clear in their cruel expressions. Here we go again I thought as the creatures were about to beat me. I could see the concern on Fernando's face as he watched them approach. He was contemplating something. Then Fernando spoke. His voice was quiet but firm. "Don't beat her. Beat me instead."

Everything stopped. Even the creatures paused.

I stared at him through the transparent wall between our cells. How could Fernando make this offer when we only met a short time ago? I had never seen anything like this. Someone choosing to suffer for me! Someone taking pain that was meant for me! In that moment, I understood something I had never grasped before, what real love actually looks like—even in the darkest place imaginable. This dark place where you had nothing to lose.

The creatures paused for just a few small moments then began to beat both of us. They beat both of us down to the ground. After they finished, they walked away telling us to be quiet. I looked at Fernando and asked "why do they do that?". He just said "I don't know".

Suddenly, and I do mean suddenly, something grabbed my attention. It grabbed my complete focus. There was light coming from one end of the room. Not the dim light from a ghostly soul nor the brighter light from a fire—this light was different. Clean. Pure. This light was white and gold together, and it was pushing back the darkness.

The creatures saw it first. Their heads snapped toward the light, and I saw something I had never seen before: fear. A very real, primal terror on their faces.

They started running. Not walking, not shuffling—running. I could see this all because of this light. Their heavy feet thundered past my cell, shaking the floor. They were running and fast as if running for their lives. There were so many of them, all fleeing from that light. Where had they all been hiding?

The light, as suddenly as it had appeared was now gone. I looked at Fernando and asked "what is going on?"

We could hear souls yelling out like a noisy crowd. I asked Fernando if he could see anything. He said "I think Jesus is here."

I asked "Jesus? Like in the Bible?".

He said "yes, yes, I think he could be coming for you".

Souls around me started shouting. "Jesus! Jesus, take me!" Their voices rose in a desperate chorus. "Please! I'm here! Take me too!" This made me wonder had he come here before and taken people out of this place.

Looking down the long hall I could see a man walking our way. I looked closer. I recognized him as that mystery man. The man who had sent me here in the first place. The man who had asked me to help his friend Fernando.

Wait! The mystery man is Jesus of the Bible!

The man walked right up to Fernando and me. He looked at me and said, "come with me. Take my hand."

Then he looked at Fernando and said, "You too Fernando".

We both held on to one of his hands. It was unclear if we were moving or if this place was moving away from us. The next thing I knew, the three of us were back at where I had been in the crash.

Fernando asked, "where are we?" I said, "this is where I died in a car crash."

Chapter Nine:

One to Heaven, One to Life

Standing at the crash site with Jesus and Fernando, I realized I had no idea what came next. I looked at Jesus wondering what would happen. He appeared to know what I was thinking. He began to tell me he was going to leave me there, take Fernando somewhere, and then come right back.

No way!

No way did I want to stay there by myself. What if those creatures came back and grabbed me? I started to protest.

"No! No! Don't leave me here."

Fernando spoke, "could we just take her with us?" Jesus was thinking and looking at me. He agreed to take me with them.

The three of us were suddenly standing at Fernando's grave. The grave he never saw because he was buried in it. It was daylight not night like at the crash. Jesus explained that we were in Buenos Aires, Argentina in 1967, just a few days after Fernando died. This mystery man, Jesus, had just taken us back in time, literally.

Jesus explained that Fernando would not be allowed to re-enter his life. He could however, go back to life in his grave to get born again and then he would go to heaven afterwards. Fernando indicated that he understood. Jesus turned to me and said "I need to leave you right here. I will take Fernando into the grave and then we will be right back. Don't worry, those creatures won't come here." I believed him but said "please hurry". I did not want to be there too long by myself. I had not forgotten what I had just been through and I was not wanting to do it again.

Jesus told Fernando to close his eyes. I could see him relax into Jesus arms as if he fell asleep. Then they both went down into the grave.

There I was, waiting. I was looking to just outside the cemetery. There was a sidewalk with people walking on it. I saw a mom with a little boy about 5 or 6 years old. For a few seconds, I thought the little boy could see me but perhaps he was looking at something past me. It appeared to be taking Fernando and Jesus so long, I began to wonder if something went wrong.

Finally, they both emerged from the grave. I felt relieved. That is when I noticed it. Fernando did not look the same. He was not all ghostly looking. He looked solid and golden like the woman in the other car at the crash. He was transformed. Jesus explained how it just took a little longer than expected.

Two glowing lightbulb people showed up just like with the woman at the crash. Jesus indicated to Fernando it was time to go. Fernando acknowledged and turned to me. He said, "thank you for coming to help me. I will see you again in heaven". He gave me a hug and turned to Jesus. "I am ready, "he said.

The lightbulb people and Fernando shot up to the sky toward a hole with light. I had seen this before with the woman in the crash. I watched until they disappeared in the hole and then the hole was gone. I still did not know how I helped Fernando but I was glad he was in heaven now.

Jesus turned to me and said, "let's get back."

Just as fast as snapping your fingers we were back at the crash. There were two lightbulb people there. Jesus instructed them to fix my body that was still in the car. They went over to the car. I watched them while Jesus stood behind me.

The two glowing beings moved to the car where my body lay. One positioned himself outside, cradling my head with his luminous hands. The other climbed partway into the wreckage. First, they straightened out my legs. Next, they removed something from my throat.

I watched, fascinated and disturbed, as they worked on my neck. The one inside appeared to be pulling at something—threads? Strings? He was gathering them, bringing the pieces together.

Then both beings worked in tandem, their hands moving in patterns I could not quite follow. It looked like they were weaving, stitching, rebuilding. They were talking to each other but I was not able to hear what they were saying. I could only see their facial expressions.

Finally, the one outside turned toward us. He gave a thumbs up. Jesus looked at me. "It's not perfect, but it should be good enough for you to live a long life. Are you ready?" I said "yes". He instructed me to relax into his arms. It was what I had just seen him do with Fernando. Everything went dark as if I fell asleep. Next thing I remember I started to open my eyes. I was on my back looking up at the back seat of the car. My first thought was, I'm back!

PART III

AFTERMATH AND RECOVERY

Chapter Ten:

The Secret I Couldn't Share

I'm back. That is all I could think as I opened my eyes and saw that back seat above me. Opening my eyes after what I had just experienced felt like waking up from the most incredible dream, except this was not a dream and I was back with memories of things no one would ever believe.

As I stared up at the seat, I tried to understand what just happened. To my right, my friend Jill was yelling for help and hitting her fist on the back window. I heard a familiar voice coming from the left side of me. I turned my head slowly to the left and saw my mom's face. It was covered in something dark – in the dim light, I could not tell what. Then I realized: blood. Her entire face was red with blood. She was saying in a very soft voice, "I can't breathe."

Panic shot through me. In the darkness, I could only see her face floating there, covered in blood. I could not see her body, could not see her shoulders or anything below. My twelve-year-old mind jumped to the worst conclusion–her head had been cut off! She was just a head!

The thought was too much. Seeing my mom like this, thinking she had been decapitated, broke something in me. Everything went black as I passed out. How much time passed I don't know, but when I opened my eyes again, my mom was not there. Where had she gone? Had the creatures come back and taken her as they had planned?

Everything was so dark in the car, I felt completely disoriented. Through the shadows, I could see Jill's mom crawling past my feet, moving from one side of the car towards the back. My eyes felt so heavy. I closed my eyes and lost consciousness again.

For the third time I regained consciousness and stayed awake this time. There was talking at the back of the car.

Jill was asking her mom, "Is she dead?".

"I don't know," her mom answered.

Jill insisted, "You can tell me the truth, I can take it."

"I don't know Jill," her mom repeated, "it's just too dark in there to tell." Jill's mom was peering into the car just as I started to move. "Oh wait, it looks like she is moving!" she said.

Jill's mom called for me to try and crawl out. A man at the window warned me to be careful of the glass everywhere. I started crawling toward the back, but my body felt heavy and exhausted. I fell to my stomach. The man suggested maybe they should not have me move, but I decided to force myself to get up and try again. I wanted out of that car, that dark enclosed space.

As I got to the back of the car, the man helped me to get the rest of the way out. I felt my feet touch the ground. Feeling dizzy at first, I regained enough strength and stood up straight. I looked directly at my friend Jill. She had one of those looks again. A look of shock, of disbelief. It was the same look she had when she had seen me in the street as a ghost just minutes before. Her look told me everything. She really had seen me dead. Neither of us said anything.

Everyone walked away, leaving me standing there at the back of our car that was now upside down, the back corner resting on the guardrail. Jill and her mom came back. Jill's mom told Jill and I to climb over the guard rail and walk past the car. There was too much glass on the ground. We got to the front of the car and climbed back over the guardrail to the road. My dad was sitting on the ground in front of the car. I sat down on the guardrail next to him.

We were waiting for first responders when my mom suddenly showed up. She appeared to be okay. Her head was not cut off after all.

My mom was worried about my two sisters. I assured her they had not been in the crash as they were in other cars that had left before us. After reminding her of this fact, she was relieved and walked away.

Although I was wearing a jacket, I was very cold. On top of it being cold, it started to rain. "Oh great," I said, "on top of everything, now we have to get rained on."

The crash had completely blocked the road and stopped any traffic from passing through. Several people that were driving on Highway 49 that had to stop, got out of their cars looking to see if they could help in any way. I remember one young man who was dressed as if he had been on a motorcycle. He walked up to me asking if he could help. I could not answer him. I was so cold and wet that I was shivering. Right away he took off his leather jacket and placed it around me. Then he looked around to see if there was anything else he could do.

Suddenly my mom showed up. Again, she asked me about my two sisters. I told her they were not there and she walked away. The man that had shared his coat asked if we should be looking for them. I explained to him that they were in other cars and not in the crash. They were most likely way down the road by this time. I turned to my dad and asked why mom would ask me a second time about the whereabouts of my sisters. He did not know. Later we would find out that my mom was walking around with a head concussion from the crash.

My mom came back a third time to ask again. This time I told my dad to tell her. Before he could explain, the wife of the man that helped us get out of the car walked up. She had been watching everything from her car and saw how wet we were getting. She offered for us to sit in her car as we waited for the first responders. My dad did not want to move as he said he was in too much pain. I thanked the man for the use of his jacket and gave it back to him. My mom and I went with the woman to her car. I was so glad to get out of the rain and to sit on a cushioned seat inside a warm dry environment.

Inside the car we talked with the woman. She and her husband had been following behind us as we were driving down the road and they saw everything. She told my mom and I that she had been praying for us after seeing the crash. She also told us that her and her husband would tell the police everything they saw. Then she asked if she could pray with us right there. My mom said yes, that she could pray with us.

The woman said a prayer. At about the same time she finished praying, the police had shown up. My mom thanked the woman and told me that we should get back out of the car and go talk to the police.

As we got out of the car, my mom started walking really fast. I could not seem to walk that fast because my right knee had a big cut on it and it was so sore. I could hardly move or bend my knee. She got away from me, so I just walked over to where my dad had been sitting. He was still there but he was now standing there with someone.

My dad was talking to a young woman. He appeared to be confused by what she was saying to him. I listened as the woman was saying how sorry she was for the crash. He asked, "Who are you? Were you in the crash?" She told us her grandmother was in the car that hit us. She lived up the street and heard the crash from her house. Since her grandmother had just left and had indicated she was not feeling well, this woman came to check if it was her grandmother.

My dad asked, "How is your grandmother? Is she okay?" The woman began to cry and said her grandmother had passed away. She was crying so much I felt I needed to tell her something. I looked her square in the eyes and grabbed her hand. "Your grandmother is in heaven now. She is okay," I told her. "How do you know this?" she asked. Then I told her how I saw two angels take her up to heaven. The woman looked shocked but hugged and thanked me for telling her.

A police officer walked up and asked if any of us were in the crash. My dad and I told her we were. The police officer told me to follow her. She walked me to a police car and had me get in the back. I climbed into the back of the police car and found my friend Jill was also sitting in the police car. She was crying and saying she thought her dad had passed away as he was still trapped in the car. We both cried and hugged each other. I told her he was not dead and everything would be okay. She asked how I knew he was not dead. I just looked at her and said, "I just know."

A few moments passed and the police officers car door opened. The police officer introduced an EMT to me and said she was going to look me over and get me to an ambulance to go to the hospital. The woman asked me if I hurt anywhere. I told her my knee and my back. She looked at my knee and back, then said she could see some scratches. Then she put a neck brace on my neck and asked if I could stand up. I stood up getting out of the police car and sat on a stretcher that had been brought close to the police car. Jill was also being put on a stretcher on the other side of the police car. Jill's mom, Jill, and myself were all transported to the hospital in the same ambulance.

Once at the hospital, I could tell that we were all in a big room together. I could hear the doctors and nurses talking to everyone, asking each one where they felt pain. Then a doctor came to me.

The doctor shined a flashlight in my eyes, then he asked if I hurt anywhere. I told him my knee and back. He looked at my knee, then turned me on my side to check my back. He said that it looked like there were just some cuts, but he would send me to get some X-rays just to make sure nothing was broken.

"One more thing", I said.

He answered, "Yes, what is it?"

"Could you turn off the lights? They are hurting my head," I asked. He told me he would get everyone taken care of and then he would turn off the lights. While I waited, I could have a pillow over my head to keep the lights from hurting me.

Finally, they got everyone processed and they turned the lights off. The doctor informed me a technician would be back to get me once the X-ray room was available. I just rested there by myself.

Jill's dad had been relocated to ICU and the others had been discharged and were waiting in another room.

My mind kept thinking about what had happened. At this point I was already starting to forget things.

Some more time passed and the doctor brought the technician in to take me to the X-ray room. The man talked to me as he pushed the bed through the hallways of the hospital. It was just useless chatter, but it felt nice. It was definitely taking my mind off thinking about the crash.

We got to the X-ray room and the man told me he would do most of the work to move me, but first he wanted to remove the neck brace. I would not need that anymore. The X-ray tech helped me onto the table. "This will just take a few minutes," he said. "Stay as still as you can."

I heard the machine click and whirl. He left the room, then came back and repositioned me. More clicks and whirls. More waiting.

Through the window, I could see him looking at something on a screen. Then another person joined him. They were both staring at the screen now, pointing at something. Their voices were muffled, but I could tell they were concerned.

The technician came back into the room, his face carefully neutral. "Just need to take a couple more x-rays," he said. More positioning. More clicking and whirling of the machines. More muffled whispering in the other room.

There was a feeling growing in the room, an atmosphere that something was wrong. I could hear another voice tell the man to check for scars. The man came back and told me he needed to check something. After checking the technician asked, "have you ever broken your neck in the past?" "No," I said. "Why?" He did not answer as he was poking around the side of my face. The man yelled out at the other voice and said, "There's nothing."

The man walked back to the other voice asking what was happening. I could hear the other person saying, "She has a broken neck, but for some reason it looks like it is healed. I'm not sure what to think. You better place the brace back on her."

That is when I realized it was not a dream. I had died because I had broken my neck and the glowing lightbulb people had fixed it. How could I tell anyone? They might think I was crazy. I knew no one would believe me. I decided I would not say anything about what happened.

The man came back to me and apologized that he had to put the brace back on my neck. He had just told me I didn't need it anymore, so I asked if there was anything wrong. He told me he could not say, but that they would talk to the doctor and get a final answer. He got me sitting up on the x-ray table and helped place me back in the original bed that he had rolled me in to the x-ray room. We then went back towards that first big room. We passed by that room to a smaller room where everyone was waiting for me, except my mom. I saw that my mom was with the doctor talking at the nurses' station. She had a very concerned look.

After a few minutes in the smaller room, my mom came and got my dad to go with her just outside the room. I knew something was wrong. There was a lot of whispering going on outside the door. I could hear them talking to the doctor. The doctor was explaining something to them. Then I heard the doctor say, "I will explain everything to her."

The doctor came in the room with another doctor and a nurse. The doctor explained that this new doctor was a special doctor. The doctor told me that I had a broken neck and that this special doctor would have to place a device on me called a halo. I knew right away what a halo was because of the football players I had seen on TV.

Earlier that year, I had watched a documentary about football players getting treatment after breaking their necks. They would have a device on that was called a halo, a metal ring screwed into their skull. A round brace holding their head completely still with shoulder pads. They could not move their heads for months. Only their eyes and mouths moved. Some had to wear them for a year.

"No way!" I yelled. "I know exactly what that is and you are NOT going to do that to me."

The doctor looked shocked. I continued to protest. "Your machine is wrong," I insisted, my voice getting louder. "I do NOT have a broken neck. My neck doesn't even hurt. You're crazy if you think I am going to let you drill into my head."

The nurse put her hand on my shoulder. "Honey, calm down. Let's just talk about this."

"There's nothing to talk about!" I started grabbing at the neck brace. "I'm taking this stupid thing off right now!" My words shocked everyone. I started to grab at the neck brace to remove it. Jill's mom and the nurse somehow calmed me down.

The nurse said, "Well let's wait just a minute." The nurse looked at the doctor and said, "She has a good point. The machine could be wrong. It wouldn't hurt to just take another X-ray."

"Yes," I said, "let's get a second opinion."

The nurse chuckled a little at me then just said, "Well you need to make a deal here. We go get another X-ray to see what is really happening, and if you still have a broken neck, you can get the halo placed, and if it is not broken, we can take off the neck brace." I agreed.

Back to the X-ray room I went, hoping that something would change. This time they took X-rays from various different angles. In addition to the new X-rays, the doctor called in an experienced specialist. We then went back to the small room.

The doctor came back with the specialist. They had looked over the new X-rays. "We have good news for you. It seems you will not need the halo device. It looks like you must have broken your neck prior to tonight's crash. The nurse will be here to remove the brace."

I felt a wave of relief. No halo. No skull screws. Then I caught my mom's expression. She was not relieved. She was suspicious and I knew why. I had never broken my neck before. At least, not that she knew about.

The nurse came and removed the neck brace and then left the room. I was relieved until I caught a glimpse of my mom still staring at me. She was mad.

"When did you break your neck?" she said.

I told her, "I didn't. Their machine is broken, not my neck."

She said, "I saw the X-rays. One mistake maybe, but the second set of X-rays were very clear. So, tell me, did you fall on your bike or skating and not tell me?" I could not tell her the truth, that I had died and lightbulb looking beings fixed my neck. She would have thought that I was the crazy one. I knew my mom very well so I just told her I did not know and that was the end of it.

Now that everything had been settled with the issue of my neck, there popped up the second issue. There had been a concern about how severe of a head injury I had obtained. The doctor concluded that it was a concussion but only under close observation would he be truly sure.

My mom however had plans of her own. She convinced the doctor that she could keep an eye on me at home. Our friend Allen was already driving back up the mountain to the hospital to pick us up except for Jill's parents. Her dad was stable but would need to remain in the hospital for a few days. Jill's mom would stay with him. My mom did not want to try to figure out an additional way to come back up the mountain and get me as we now had no car.

The doctor was concerned about how my mom could take care of me. She had three broken ribs, a concussion of her own, and my mom was not a doctor. The doctor told her a list of things she would need to do to make sure I was going to be ok. My mom was insistent and told the doctor she could handle everything. Reluctantly, the doctor agreed to discharge me.

Shortly after the decision was made, Allen showed up. We all walked outside towards Allen's station wagon. Fear suddenly gripped me. No way did I want to get into another car. What if it happened again? I never wanted to see that awful place again. I started to panic and stated we should all go back into the hospital. I was just not ready to get into another car. My protests were met with coaxing and reasoning of how it would be so quick to just drive home. I gave in realizing that I could not win this battle.

Chapter Eleven:

Hidden and Forgotten

The car was quiet during the entire drive home. It was so late and we were all so tired. It felt as if we got home really fast. Once inside my dad went straight to bed. My mom told me I could go to bed but I could not go to sleep because of the head injury. What? How was I supposed to do that? Now I wished I had been allowed to stay at the hospital.

After several hours of my mom waking me up at just the right moment when I was almost asleep, she decided I had passed the time that she felt would be dangerous. She let me fall asleep. As soon as I fell asleep, I began to dream but my dream was not a normal dream. As I slept, I replayed the whole car crash event. I was in the awful place with those creatures and the boss that wanted my mom.

Suddenly, I was awakened by my mom. She was standing over the top of me. I asked her what she was doing. I thought she had said I could go to sleep. She told me she had woken me up because I was screaming in my sleep. She asked if I was having a bad dream. I told her yes. She had me get up and tell her the dream.

We went to the living room and I told her about the dream, knowing it was a replay of the night's events, at least the parts where I was in that awful place. I told her of the creatures taking me to a scary place where their was a boss and of meeting a man named Fernando and the very dark room of cells. Once I finished, all she had to say was, "well it was only a dream and you are safe at home". I did not tell her I had actually experienced all of this. She was convinced it was only a dream.

Saturday went by and Sunday morning came fast. We were still recovering but by now my head was really hurting. The pain in my head was getting worse as the day went on until I felt I could no longer stand it anymore. Something felt very wrong. "Mom, can we call 911. My head really hurts." She told me it was expected that my head might hurt 'a little'.

The pain I was experiencing in my head had grown and was not 'a little' pain. I am not able to explain why but I really wanted to see a doctor right away. Mom insisted I had a doctor appointment Monday and I could wait until then to see the doctor. My grandmother would be picking us up in the morning. Then she instructed me to go lay down and rest.

Monday rolled around and I was off to the doctor appointment. My head had stopped hurting and everything felt good except now I could not remember what happened in the crash.

At the doctor's office, I told the doctor how my head was hurting so bad the day before. She decided I needed a head scan. We went down the hall to get the test done then came back to her office. She told me that there was evidence my head had swelled and had bled perhaps all weekend but appeared to have stopped now. She decided that I needed to do a memory test and find out if there was any damage.

The memory test revealed I had an M4 traumatic brain injury, or what is called a TBI. As a result, I was also experiencing amnesia – but not just one kind. The doctor explained that I had lost memories from before the crash and was also having trouble forming and keeping new memories. She said one type was related specifically to not remembering the crash itself, which she thought might come back someday. The other memory problems, she warned, could be permanent, the one of forming and keeping memories. I felt overwhelmed with emotions, knowing I would not be able to remember everything, left me worried. How was I going to manage?

After thirty seven years and without having copies of my medical records, I do not remember the exact terms she used. What I do remember clearly is the reality of it: I could not remember much of my life before the crash. I also had no memory of the crash or what happened to me during the crash. Going forward in life, my ability to form and keep new memories was severely impacted. Day by day, my life became altered away from what we call a 'normal' life.

Chapter Twelve:

A Stranger in My Own Life

The X-rays showed my neck had been perfectly healed. The brain scans showed the bleeding had stopped. My cuts were healing and by every medical measure, I was recovering. My doctor was pleased. My parents were relieved. What no test could measure was that the most important parts of who I was had been completely erased.

All the facts were there—my age, my school, my family, my friends—but the images that should have connected me to those facts had vanished completely. I was a functioning stranger, appearing normal to others since I knew the facts, but internally I felt no emotional connection to my own life.

The informational side of my memory was working quite well. This side of the brain is usually referred to as the left side and helps to retain data and facts. I knew I had been in a terrible crash but I had no visual memory of it. When asked what I remembered it was all factual and it was the facts that I had been told after the crash. There were 3 cars. One car hit us head on because the driver had a heart attack while driving. The third car hit the first car that was in a spin after it had hit us. I had no real memory of the events and that included the part where I died and came back. I did not remember the aftermath at the crash scene or any of the events that happened at the hospital.

Some movies and TV shows have been made over the years that portray someone that has amnesia. These movies or shows usually have the person forgetting their name and where they are and who the important people are in their life before they had the memory loss. This was not my experience. I knew my name and who everyone was around me. In fact, my left-brain function appeared to be sharper than average.

The right brain function was the challenge. This side of the brain holds emotions and images. I appeared to have a disconnect with the images of my memory and my emotions were all over the place and out of control a lot of the time.

This emotional change was so significant that I started to lose friends. Some people just could not handle seeing me so different. I was fearful most of the time and I became a recluse. Whenever there were conversations about things of the past, I was full of questions of when, where, and why. After a while, that kind of questioning everything can be too much for some people, especially family and friends.

One day after a couple years had gone by since the crash, I was at Jill's house hanging out. Jill had been telling everyone all along that she saw me as a ghost standing outside the car the night of the crash. This day at her house, she was getting into an argument with her mom on the subject. I remember how they were going round and round. Jill's mom pointed at me and told Jill if I was dead, I would not be standing right there. Jill's come back was that somehow, I came back to life. Her mom went into her room and shut the door. Then Jill went to her own room and shut the door.

It reminded me of a television show called Moonlighting.

There I was still standing in the hall not sure what to do. After a few minutes I knocked on Jill's door and asked if I could come in. Jill opened the door and pulled me in shutting the door behind me.

If only I could get my memory back all this could get cleared up. "Jill," I said, "I wish I could remember so you and your mom wouldn't have to fight about it. I am so sorry I can't remember." Jill placed her hands on my shoulders and said, "this is not your fault, this is between me and my mom. You don't have to feel sorry."

We decided to go get popsicles from the garage freezer. We pulled out the popsicles and went to the kitchen. Jill's mom came in and the tension was immediate.

"Jill, we've talked about this," her mom said, her voice tight. "You need to stop telling people you saw her as a ghost."

"But I did see her!" Jill's voice was rising. "I'm not making it up!"

"Honey, you were traumatized. The crash was terrible. Sometimes our minds—"

"My mind is fine!" Jill interrupted. "I know what I saw!"

"Jill." Her mom's voice had an edge now. "Enough."

"No! Not enough!" Jill was almost yelling. "She was dead! I checked, twice! No heartbeat, no breathing! Then she was standing outside the car!"

"That's impossible and you know it!"

"It happened!"

I stood there holding my popsicle, watching them fight about what had or had not happened to me as if I was not even there. The rage building in me was not about defending Jill or her mom – it was about the noise, the conflict, the overwhelming feeling that I could not handle any of it.

What happened next was pretty wild. I had very little control over my emotions and started yelling at both of them. "That's it. I am done with this. I am calling my mom to come get me and I am never coming over here again. This crash has ruined everything." I called my mom and told her to come get me right away.

The atmosphere was quiet as we waited for my mom to show up. Jill's mom told me she wanted me to wait inside when my mom got there so they could talk for a minute.

Once my mom was there, Jill's mom went outside. The two of them were talking near the front door. First, they were quiet but after a few minutes they were both yelling at each other. I could hear my mom say "you raise your daughter the way you want to raise her and I will raise my daughter the way I want to raise her." The door opened and my mom told me to come. We left on very bad terms. I suddenly lost my best friend.

In the car drive home, I asked my mom what happened. She did not want to talk about it. All she told me was that Jill's mom thought I should go to see a counselor and my mom disagreed. I thought what good that would do since I did not remember anything so what would I have to talk about.

We stopped going to church. That started another downwards slope in our lives. Since most of our friends were at church, we suddenly did not have friends to see and be around anymore. I felt completely disconnected from faith, not knowing that I had already met Jesus and been rescued by Him.

More time passed and I wondered if I would ever get my memory back. I started to forget about my friend Jill.

One day my mom and I were driving down a street near where Jill lived. I asked my mom why we never see them. My mom looked at me and said "don't you remember." I answered, "remember what?" My mom explained how I got in a fight with Jill and her mom. I had told them I did not want to be friends anymore. I was shocked. I did not remember doing such a thing and had an overwhelming sense that I needed to make it right. I told my mom to turn the car around and go to Jill's house. At first, she did not want to but I insisted that I needed to go. Mom turned the car and went back. She said she was going to stay in the car.

When we got to their house, I ran to the door, knocking as loud as I could. No one answered. It appeared no one was home. I went to the car and asked my mom if we could wait a few minutes. We waited but no one came so we left. I asked my mom if we could try again another day. She agreed but soon I forgot all about it and we never went back.

Driving away from Jill's house that day, I wondered if I would ever get my memory back. I asked my mom and she just reminded me that the doctor stated my memory would come back at some point. "But it's been over two years! When is it coming back?" I asked. I was frustrated living like this. My mom just said, "remember the doctor did not know how long it would take. You have to be patient." I came to the conclusion that very moment that I would never get my memory back. After two years of people asking "Do you remember yet?" and me always saying no, I made that decision. I was never getting my memories back.

Every time someone mentioned the crash, I would feel this pressure – like I should remember, like I was failing by not remembering. The doctor said the memories might come back someday, but two years felt like forever when you are fourteen.

So, I stopped thinking about it. Stopped asking questions. Stopped trying to piece together what happened. It was easier to just accept that part of my life was gone.

I did not know that in blocking out the memories of the crash, that I was also blocking out the most important spiritual experience I had ever had. I did not understand that I was forgetting about Jesus. My memory was so lost to me from that point on I even forgot I had amnesia. It is like I blocked it from my mind.

Moving forward my life was just me living in the present moment. I could not remember most things and I did not seem to care anymore. To this day I still do not remember much about my high school years. It is all a big blur. Years passed with me in this haze or emotional fog. I went through the motions of high school – classes, homework, basic social interactions – but formed no deep connections or lasting memories.

Chapter Thirteen:

Disbelief and Curiosity

My aunt started asking me to visit her church the summer before my senior year in high school. Every weekend, like clockwork: "Want to come to church with me Sunday?"

"No thanks," I would say.

"There are young people your age there," she would reply.

"I'm not interested," I would state, thinking she would stop asking.

"The worship is really different from what you're used to," she would coax.

"I don't want to go to church," I would flat out state.

This went on for weeks. I started getting annoyed. Didn't she understand I did not care about church? I did not care about much of anything.

She kept asking. Every single weekend. Looking back now, I see God's hand in her persistence. At the time, I just thought she was being stubborn and not hearing me.

After asking several times she told me of a boy she wanted me to meet at her church. She thought that if I wanted to meet him, I would have to go to church with her. She convinced me by stating I could have a nice boyfriend and that she thought he was cute. I only agreed because she really talked him up as a really great guy. She would pick me up the following Sunday.

Almost five years earlier, my family had stopped going to church entirely. Now here I was, eighteen years old, walking back into a church not seeking faith but hoping for a boyfriend. I had no idea I was about to experience my first genuine emotion since the crash.

That Sunday morning, I woke up regretting my decision. I did not want to go to church. I definitely did not want to meet some boy my aunt had picked out for me but she was already on her way to pick me up.

The drive felt long. My aunt was talking about the church, how different it was, how I would really like it. I barely listened. I was thinking about how soon I could leave, how to politely meet this guy and then never come back.

"Just give it a chance," my aunt said as we pulled into the parking lot of the junior college. I looked at the building. A church meeting in a college lobby. This was already weird. What had I gotten myself into? This guy had better be worth it.

We arrived late but my aunt said no one would notice. They would be singing songs at the beginning and not watching the doors. It felt strange to me how excited she was about church. Well maybe this guy was really great. I was about to find out.

We went inside and the music was very loud like a rock concert. I was used to churches that just had a piano and an organ. This was drums and guitars. In addition, everyone had their arms up in the air. This was really weird to me. We quickly found some seats but did not sit down as everyone was standing. I wondered if this was really church. What had my aunt brought me to?

The second thing I noticed was a feeling in the atmosphere. It was not like anything I had felt before. It was peaceful and joyful. My thought was these people must be on some cool drug. Literally, I thought that. At that moment, I failed to realize the fact that I would have had to be taking the same drug as they did in order to feel this feeling.

The service was over before I knew it and people started to come around to say hi to my aunt. She introduced me to different people but I was curious who was the guy I was supposed to meet. I started to think it was all a trick.

I said to my aunt, "There is no guy for me to meet is there?".

"Oh yes there is a guy," she said looking around. "His name is Dave. Let me see, I know he should be here because he never misses a Sunday."

She was still looking around when a man walked up named Rick. He was the youth leader. He was inviting me to this youth meeting later in the week. I was not sure as I did not drive and would not know how to get there. Of course, my aunt had a way to fix that. She would take me if I really wanted to go. I agreed only because I thought it would get me out of the house for a while. It was all set.

Finally, the guy Dave came over. He was ok but I could not help but think my aunt just chose him on the spot. He did not seem to know I was there to meet him.

"Dave, this is my niece," my aunt said. "This is her first time here."

"Cool," he said. "What did you think?"

I did not know how to answer him. Weird? Intense? Different? "It was... interesting," I finally said. This still felt like a set up but I was so curious about what I felt that day.

On the drive home, my aunt asked what I thought.

"It was different," I said.

"Different good or different bad?"

I thought about it. The music had been overwhelming. The people felt a little too enthusiastic. Dave was ok, I guess. I was not sure he was going to become my boyfriend the way my aunt was convinced he would.. Yet that feeling, that peaceful, joyful atmosphere. I could not shake it. I wanted to feel it again, to understand what it was.

"Different… interesting," I finally said. "I think I'll come back next week."

My aunt tried to hide her smile, but I could see it. She was already planning, already hoping. I just wanted to figure out what that feeling was. Maybe it was just the music. Maybe it was something else.

High school started shortly after this first time in church. For several months I went to this church and the youth night. In October, I invited a long-time neighbor friend to go with me to the youth night. We were told we would have pizza. My friend decided she would like to come with me. That night one of the women that helped on youth night started to talk to my friend about finding Jesus. By the end of the night my friend had decided to become a follower of Jesus.

Months went by and I was having this growing feeling something was wrong with me. I kept asking Rick, the youth leader, questions about the bible. He always appeared to have pretty good answers. How did he know so much about God? He would read different things in the Bible. They all felt new as if I had never heard them before. I started reading the Bible but nothing made sense.

It was Easter 1994 and the young adult's group were doing a short skit Saturday night. They played a song about the prodigal son by an artist named Keith Green. While the song played, they acted out the story.

Before we went to watch the skit, Rick told me to watch it as the guy playing the dad was God and the guy playing the son was me. I looked at Rick and said, "what are you talking about?" He just looked at me and said "you will understand as you watch the skit."

We watched the skit and I thought about what Rick told me. God was the dad and I was the son. I analyzed the story. To me the son had run away from home in a sense. The interesting part was when the son came back and the dad was not mad at him. He was just welcoming and loving. So how did this relate to me? How could you run away from God's home and come back?

The next morning was Easter Sunday and the young adults did the skit again. I felt bothered all day. Why did this skit bother me so much?

The youth group spent the day at my aunts. Rick drove everyone home. He took me home last. When we got to my house we sat in the car. I told Rick I was worried about where I would go if I died, if I would make it to heaven. I still had no memory of the events of the crash. Rick stated we could pray and I could find out. At first, I said 'ok' and then I quickly said 'no'. What was happening to me? I was not usually indecisive.

Rick paused. He said, "how about this? You think about what you want God to do for you. Once you have something, I will pray then you can pray. Ok?" I agreed and thought, what did I want God to do for me. Well, I wanted him to love me like what I saw in the skit. I told Rick I was ready. He told me not to tell him what I wanted God to do for me. He said that it was just between God and me. Rick started to pray.

As Rick prayed, I began to feel a presence of a person. I had my eyes closed and could see a vision of a face. It was a kind and happy face. At that moment I felt this face was God and he was telling me he loved me. It got to my turn to pray but I was crying at this point and all I could say was Jesus.

After a few minutes I looked up at Rick. I shouted, "he's real. Jesus is real and I'm going to heaven."

PART IV

HEALING AND DISCOVERY

Chapter Fourteen

Awakening Without Remembering

Had the world always been this beautiful? Walking to school that Monday morning after finding Jesus, the colors around me appeared deeper, more alive. The sky was bluer than before. The leaves on the trees were not just green—they were vibrant, almost glowing. Even the birds appeared more colorful than I had ever noticed. Everything looked as if viewed through a dirty window for my entire lifetime, and someone had finally removed the dirty glass.

The changes went beyond just colors. Food tasted better – like my taste buds had been muted and suddenly turned back on. Music moved in ways it had not before. Even pain felt different – more real, more present, but somehow more bearable because it was actually felt instead of just numbly existing through it.

For seven years, my life had been a fog, disconnected from everything and everyone. Now it was like someone had opened windows that were not known to be closed. Fresh air was rushing in, and breathing felt possible again.

This new life was so exciting. The desire to know as much as possible about Jesus drove me to attend every church meeting, daily Bible reading, and participation in every youth event. Rick was very helpful as someone who could answer questions, and believe me, there were a lot of questions. Others from the church began to help too, all so supportive in my start of living as a follower of Jesus. Still, I had no memory of personally meeting Jesus that night years ago when the crash happened.

Trying to understand the Bible and remember where to find specific passages was very challenging. The amnesia had been completely forgotten. A solution emerged: using color pencils to draw pictures in the Bible that would give clues as to what each section was about. For example, in John where it talked about Jesus being placed in a tomb, I would place a small tomb over those few verses. This really helped because when flipping through pages and seeing a drawing, the memory of what it discussed would return.

The memory issues made being a new follower of Jesus frustrating. Breakthroughs in understanding something – grace, or faith, or the Holy Spirit – would bring such excitement. Then the next day, the lesson would be forgotten. Starting over meant re-reading the same passages, asking Rick the same questions I had asked before.

He never appeared annoyed, which was amazing. His patient explanations would come again, sometimes using the exact same words. Looking back now, he must have realized how many times we'd had the same conversation.

The first few months' passed and high school graduation arrived. The decision was made to take a gap year and figure out what to do with this new life. During this time, every Saturday I brought the same question to Mom: did she want to go to church? My aunt had done it successfully with me, so perhaps it might work with Mom too.

Every week she said no, but that did not stop me from asking. This went on for months.

Finally, one Sunday in November, the decision was made not to ask her. Getting ready as usual to wait for my aunt to pick me up, mom suddenly jumped up off the couch and started heading to her room. When I asked if something was wrong, she said no but that she had decided she wanted to come to my church, though she wanted to drive herself.

The shock was overwhelming. I called my aunt while mom was getting ready, she was also shocked but worried that my mom would change her mind and my ride would be missed. She was right to be concerned as my mom had not been to church in almost 6 years, but I assured her that my mom was serious and that we would see my aunt at church.

My mom loved her first time at my church and decided to make it her new church. Perhaps it was because these were all new people who did not know our past. A few weeks later, dad came too. We were back in church, developing our relationship with God and a new community.

We were rebuilding, not the same as before – none of us were the same people we had been before the crash. We were together in this, all of us seeking God, all of us starting fresh in a community that did not know our history.

The details of the next thirty years would be wonderful to share. What it was like growing in faith, how my relationship with Jesus deepened, the challenges faced, the victories celebrated. The truth is, those three decades exist in fragments rather than the clear scenes shared so far. The amnesia that erased the death and rescue did not stop affecting me after the crash. The ability to form and retain memories remained compromised, even as a life of faith was being built in me.

What is known is this: I walked with Jesus for thirty years without knowing He had already rescued me. Loving Him without remembering Fernando's sacrifice or the lightbulb people who healed my broken neck. Everything I had built as a follower of Jesus rested on a foundation that could not be remembered. My life was simply a day-to-day life.

Chapter Fifteen:

The Healing That Started Everything

In 2024, I started taking a class that taught about healing. In this class there was teaching and then small groups that talked and implemented what had been taught. After several weeks, one night the small group leader Sandra asked if any of us had a need for physical healing.

After the traumatic brain injury, daily head pain became a permanent companion. Most days it was manageable. Then there were days when the pain became so bad that lying down was the only option. It was just part of my life, a permanent reminder of the crash that could not be remembered.

I had accepted it. This was just how things were. The pain had been there so long I barely even thought about it anymore unless it got really bad.

Speaking up about this head pain, Sandra and the group decided to pray for me. As the group prayed, I felt a strange sensation in my head. It was a melting feeling. It started at the top and went all the way to my neck. When the sensation stopped, I no longer had head pain. This was wonderful because I had suffered for so long.

After I was healed of the head pain, I could not help but tell all my friends. When I shared how I had gotten the head pain and now it was gone I would always state that I had no memory of the crash.

One of the people I told of my healing was a friend named Anna. After telling Anna of my healing and not remembering the crash, she said to me, "the reason you don't remember is because you died and went to hell and Jesus brought you back". I looked at her and stated that just because I could not remember does not mean that is what happened. I had only known Anna for a few years so there was no way for her to know what happened to me. On two other occasions as I told my healing story, Anna would say it again.

The second time Anna said it, I was more direct. "Please don't say that, Anna. You don't know what happened," I explained.

"I do know," she said, her voice gentle but firm.

"You were not there," I insisted. "Nobody knows what happened except me, and I don't remember."

She would not back down. The third time she said it, I got angry. "Stop. Just stop saying that."

She looked at me with this expression I could not quite read. Not hurt. Not defensive. More like… she was waiting for something. Like she knew something I did not, and she was just waiting for me to figure it out. I had no idea she was speaking prophetic truth. I had no idea that in just a few months, I would discover she had been right all along.

There was also something that I did not realize had happened that night at class when my head was healed. I had been healed of more than the head pain. Memories I had not been able to access for 37 years were beginning to surface – fragments at first, then more. The next four or five months would answer the question I had carried since the crash: What really happened to me that night? The answer would be more extraordinary than anything I could have imagined, and would force me to confront an impossible truth: Anna had been right all along.

Chapter Sixteen:

Piecing Together the Past

The same healing class where my head pain had vanished was also teaching something else. Trauma buries itself, and healing requires going after it at the root. The method they used was called the prayer model, and I was about to discover just how deep my roots went.

Our teacher explained that traumatic events often create lies we come to believe as truth. To be truly healed, we needed to identify them and replace them with the truth. We also needed to forgive, not by confronting people or having difficult conversations, but through a private heart decision to release them. Forgiveness is for our freedom.

As I worked through these concepts, something in my mind began to shift. I had no idea that this healing class would become the key to unlocking 37 years of buried memory.

Jeanine came into my life in 2018, a woman trained in inner healing who would later become a close friend. Over the years, as she helped me work through various life issues, we developed a strong friendship. When the crash memories began returning in 2024, Jeanine was the person I turned to for help. I would share each fragment I remembered, and together we would search for what might be blocking a fuller memory—lies I believed about the trauma and forgiveness I was holding back. Every piece we processed appeared to unlock more. Jeanine would guide me through prayer, helping me identify where I felt stuck. We would pray through each fragment, asking God to reveal lies and bring truth.

Sometimes I would feel immediate relief. Other times, we would have to work through multiple layers before a blocked memory would fully release its hold on me. In between sessions, I worked to arrange the fragments in sequential order, trying to transform the disjointed pieces into one continuous memory from start to finish.

It started with headlights. Three days after the healing of the head pain in the healing class, I suddenly saw them—headlights aimed at our car. Then the image was gone. A few days later, another fragment appeared, that of being thrown around inside the car.

Then another piece. The memories were coming back in jumps, like cut scenes in a movie, when they should have been continuous. Each fragment forced me to ask: What happened next? What am I missing between these pieces? I had no idea where filling in these gaps would eventually lead.

As I walked through the healing process, I struggled to identify the lies I believed, so I began with forgiveness. First, I forgave my sister for not following the rules and taking my seat in Allen's car for the return trip back home that night. The delay had taken so much more time, all the cars in our caravan would have been past this woman's entry to Highway 49. Then I forgave the woman who hit us for choosing to drive when she was not well—for not staying at her granddaughter's home with her family as they had suggested.

Once I completed the forgiveness work, I was able to dig deeper and uncover the buried lies beneath. Most centered on "what if" scenarios: What if we had not gone that night? What if my sister had behaved? What if the woman had not driven? The thing about "what ifs" and false guilt is that they are not reality. We cannot change past decisions, and trauma was not my fault.

There were deeper lies too—lies about my worth, about deserving what happened, about being somehow responsible. I believed I was broken beyond repair and that I was not normal. Bad things always happen to me. This ruined my family's life. This ruined many of my friendships. No one could understand me, so why try to connect? All of these were lies.

Week after week and little by little I began to heal. My memories were returning at a rapid pace. From February 2024 to May 2024, I pieced together the events of the crash itself.

The process was exhausting. Each memory brought emotional weight—grief for what happened, anger at the circumstances, fear of what I might remember next. Some days I wanted to stop, to leave the past buried. Some days I thought I should never have remembered any of it because I was feeling as if I was worse off. But something drove me forward. I needed to know the complete truth, even if it was painful.

The emotional toll of the memory work surprised me. I thought remembering would bring relief—finally knowing what happened after so many years of blankness. Instead, it was exhausting work, with each memory brought fresh grief. I grieved for my twelve-year-old self who had experienced such trauma. I grieved for my family who had nearly lost me. I grieved for Jill, who had witnessed my death and carried that burden alone for decades with no one believing her, not even me.

Some memories brought physical reactions too. I would remember being thrown around inside the car and my body would tense up, bracing for impact even though I was sitting safely on my couch. I would remember the fear and my heart would race. My brain could not always distinguish between simply remembering the trauma compared to actually experiencing it again.

March turned to April, then May. The fragments kept coming—sometimes daily, sometimes with gaps of several days. I started keeping notes, trying to piece together the timeline. The more I remembered about the crash itself, the more I sensed there was something beyond the physical trauma I could not yet access.

By mid-May, I had assembled most of the crash sequence. I understood what happened physically—the collision, the flipping, my injuries, and the moments before everything went dark. There was a gap I could not explain. What happened in the back of that destroyed car during the time I was unconscious?

The third Friday in May, I attended a worship night at church, not expecting anything in particular. The music was wonderful. I was standing there, eyes closed, just trying to feel God's presence.

During the service, a memory broke through that was different from all the crash fragments I had been piecing together. I suddenly remembered dying—not almost dying, but actually dying and falling out of my body onto the paved road. This was not just another fragment of the physical crash. This was something else entirely. I was remembering standing on the Highway looking down at my hands.

My heart was pounding. Around me, worship continued, but I was somewhere else entirely. I could see it—actually see it—my ghostly looking body standing on that dark road, watching the car settle upside down.

The music faded into background noise as the memory kept playing. This was not a crash memory. This was something that happened after the impact of the crash. This was me, dead, outside my body, wondering how I had gotten there.

Jeanine was at that worship night. When it was over, we went out to my car. There I told her what I was remembering.

In the car, the words tumbled out. "I died. I actually died. I wasn't just unconscious or in a coma—I left my body. I was standing on the road, looking at myself in the wreckage."

Jeanine listened intently; her expression serious. "What else do you remember?"

"That's it so far. Just that moment of standing there, confused about how I got out of the car. But Jeanine…" I paused, trying to find words for what I was feeling.

"This is different from the other memories. The crash memories feel traumatic, but this feels… I don't know how to describe it. Real in a different way. Like I'm remembering something that actually happened to my spirit, not just my body."

"What do you want to do?" she asked.

I explained to Jeanine, "I need to pray through this. I need to know what comes next in this memory. If I died and left my body, something must have happened while I was out there."

We prayed together, asking God to reveal whatever I needed to know, to bring truth and healing, and to help me process whatever was coming. When we finished, I felt both peace and uneasiness.

On the drive home that night, I could not help but think of Anna's words from earlier in the year. "You died and went to hell and Jesus brought you back." I had been so angry when she said it that third time. I was so certain she was wrong, speaking about things she could not possibly know.

But now… now I had just remembered dying. Leaving my body. Standing outside the car, separate from my physical body. If that part was true—if I really had died—could the rest of what Anna said also be true?

My hands gripped the steering wheel tighter. Hell. Jesus. Rescue. It sounded impossible. Crazy. The kind of thing people make up or imagine or hallucinate.

The memory of standing on that road did not feel made up. It felt as real as driving that car right then, as real as anything I had ever experienced. Even more real because it was so vivid, so detailed, and so completely unlike anything my imagination could have created.

If I died, where did I go? What happened during the time I was gone? And if Jesus really did bring me back, why could not I remember Him?

The questions swirled as I drove through the darkness. I did not have answers yet, not yet, but I had a feeling they were coming.

I pulled into my driveway and sat in the car for a moment, engine off, surrounded by silence. One memory had broken through tonight—me, standing on that road, dead but somehow still conscious.

I knew this was just the beginning. More memories were waiting, and based on what I had already pieced together, these additional memories to come were going to challenge everything I thought I knew about life, death, and what lies beyond.

Anna had been right about the dying part. I had a sinking feeling she was about to be proven right about the rest.

Chapter Seventeen:

Remembering the Other Side

Anna's words had irritated me for months. "You died and went to hell and Jesus brought you back." Now, after the healing prayer, I could not stop thinking about them. Now that I was starting to remember things, her impossible claim felt less impossible.

A few weeks after that Friday worship night when I remembered I died, I found myself in a Sunday morning service when flash images began surfacing—first the creatures, then fire. My heart started racing. These were not the crash memories. These were something else entirely, something impossible.

Then I saw cells. Transparent walls. Souls trapped inside. Just fragments of images, but enough for me to recognize—these were memories of hell.

The Sunday morning worship continued around me, but I was frozen, trying to process what I was seeing. Then a sudden urgency overtook me: I had to find Anna. I needed her to confirm what she had told me, to validate that these fragments were real.

Deep inside, I felt that if Anna could verify her words, I would know this was truly happening. I realize now I was in shock from the memories coming up to the surface.

Shock is a strange thing. For me it came with a deep inner rejection of the truth. Nonetheless, I tracked down Anna.

When I found Anna, I pulled her aside outside the church building. My hands were shaking. Panic rising in my chest, I asked, "Anna, did you say the reason I could not remember the crash was because I died and went to hell and Jesus brought me back?" She went still. For a few minutes she said nothing. Then she removed her sunglasses and stared directly into my eyes. Her answer was not what I expected. Anna simply said, "You remembered." I was still panicking—so much that I asked again, needing to hear it clearly. This time she answered: "Yes."

"How could this be? How could this be true?" I replied in a way that was more like thinking out loud. Anna grabbed my hands. "You're okay. Let me pray for you." She began praying right there, her voice steady and sure. "Father, thank You for bringing these memories back. Thank You for trusting her with this testimony. Jesus, help her process what she's remembering. Take away the fear and panic. Remind her that You were there, that You rescued her, that she's safe now. Let her know this story is not a burden—it is a gift. A gift to her and a gift she will share with others who need to hear it." As her words washed over me, the panic slowly loosened its grip. I was not fine, not even close, but I could breathe again.

Later that week, on a Friday I had off from work, the memories came flooding back—much more of the experience in hell. As I pieced things together, I remembered one name: Fernando Paternoster. Could I find him online?

I sat with my phone Google app, staring at the search bar. This was the test. If Fernando was real, if I could find evidence he actually existed, then I would have to accept that everything else was real too. The creatures. The cells. Hell itself. Jesus rescuing both Fernando and myself. It felt like a long shot, but if I could find even a picture, it would prove to me he was real. He had lived and died before I was ever born, so there was no other way to verify his existence.

My hands hovered over the phone's keyboard. Part of me did not want to search. As long as I did not look, I could still tell myself this might not be real.

But I had to know.

Regardless of the odds, I opened Google and typed his name, then clicked on the images tab.

There he was—so many pictures.

Young, in soccer clothing. Older, wearing glasses. Then I found the older photos without glasses, and my breath caught. It was him. Exactly as I remembered him. The same kind face. The same gentle expression. The man I had met in that cell, who had offered to take my beating, who I had helped Jesus rescue.

He was real. He had actually existed. Born in Argentina. Played soccer in the 1928 Olympics. Won a silver medal. Died June 6, 1967, at age 64. Everything he had told me was true.

I started crying right there. If Fernando was real, then everything else was real too. Everything started to sink in deep—the reality of my situation. This was the moment when denial could no longer protect me from what I knew was real. I really had died. I really had been to hell. Jesus really had rescued us both — Fernando Paternoster and me.

There was no more room for doubt.

Chapter Eighteen:

The Weight of Knowing

Finding out Fernando was real and what I experienced was real created a great deal of emotional distress. At this moment of emotional distress, I suddenly received a text from my friend Sonja. She was just thinking about me and wanted to see how I was doing. Sonja had no idea what had been happening over the last few months, so her timing was truly God-sent. I texted back that I was not doing well. Sensing something was really wrong, she called me right away. The moment I answered, she asked, "What's wrong?" I burst into tears. Through the sobbing, I told her I had died and gone to hell.

"What?" was all she said.

"I know how it sounds," I sobbed. "I know it sounds crazy. But it's true. I have proof. I found him—Fernando, the man I met there. He's real. He really existed. And

Anna knew. She told me months ago and I got so angry, but she was right."

"Slow down," Sonja said gently. "Take a breath. Are you safe? Are you okay?"

"I don't know," I admitted. "I don't know if I'm okay. This is too much. It's too big. I died, Sonja. I actually died, and I went to this horrible place, and Jesus came to get me, and I forgot all of it for 37 years. Why did I forget? Why am I remembering now?"

"Where are you right now?" she asked.

"At home," I replied.

"Okay. Do you want to come over? Right now. Can you drive? Are you okay to drive?"

I took a shaky breath. "Yes. I think so."

"Then come over. We'll talk through this together. You're not alone in this, okay? Whatever this is, we'll figure it out together."

Knowing I needed more than a phone call, and hearing the genuine care in her voice, I told her yes—I could leave in a few minutes.

She lived only fifteen minutes away. I pulled myself together the best I could and drove to Sonja's home.

Once I got to Sonja's, we sat down at her kitchen island and I told her everything I could remember. The words poured out—no longer organized or coherent, just the raw experience tumbling out.

I told her about falling out of my body and standing on the dark highway, confused about how I got there. About the creatures grabbing me and carrying me into the forest, into darkness so complete I could not see anything. About the elevator going down, down, down into the earth.

I described the fire pit where souls were being pushed in repeatedly, burning to skeletons, climbing out, getting back in line to have this done to them again. The fire river with people chained to the cliffs. The vast number of buildings full of cells where souls were imprisoned.

"There was this man in the cell next to me," I said. "Fernando. He had been there for twenty years without knowing it. Time doesn't work the same there. He had thought it had been maybe five years, but it was twenty, and when I told everyone, it was 1987, they all panicked because they realized how long they'd been trapped."

Sonja listened, her eyes wide, but never once did she look at me like I was crazy. She just nodded, taking it all in.

"Then Jesus came," I continued. "He walked right up to my cell and told Fernando and I to take His hand. He rescued both of us—Fernando and me. He took Fernando to heaven, and He brought me back to my body at the crashed car."

At that time, I still had gaps in the memories, but enough to give her a clear picture of what happened. This was the first time I had shared that fateful night with anyone with this much detail. She was amazed. Never once did she treat me like I was crazy. She believed me and supported me completely.

Then I asked if she wanted to see a picture of Fernando Paternoster—the man I met in hell. She looked at me, shocked. "How did you find him?" I told her I had just searched Google. I pulled up a photo on my phone and showed her.

We talked for a long time, until the weight began to lift and I felt calm again. Then I went home.

Driving home, the panic had faded but a new weight had settled in its place. The weight of knowledge. The weight of experience. The weight of a story that appeared impossible but was undeniably true.

Why? Why had God brought these memories back after 37 years? I had built an entire life of faith without them. I had followed Jesus for three decades without remembering He had already rescued me once before. Was my remembering necessary? Was there a reason I had to forget?

Why remember now? Why not take those experiences, this secret to my grave? Why put me through the trauma of reliving hell, of processing Fernando's sacrifice, of confronting the reality of what lies beyond death?

The questions haunted me as I pulled into my driveway: Was this story meant to stay private? Bury it again, this time consciously? Or was there a reason—a purpose—for these memories surfacing now? I had proof—Anna's prophetic words, Fernando's real existence. But what was I supposed to do with this knowledge?

PART V

TRANSFORMATION AND PURPOSE

Chapter Nineteen

Finding New Purpose

After the memories returned, I wrestled with what to do. The questions kept me awake at night. Should I keep this private? Would anyone believe me? What if people thought I was crazy?

The fear was real. I imagined people whispering behind my back, questioning my mental state, distancing themselves from 'the woman who thinks she went to hell.' I imagined losing friendships, being dismissed, becoming known as 'crazy' instead of credible.

Underneath all the questions going through my mind about the impact of my story was one persistent truth, Jesus is real. Hell is also real, and people need to know. Not because I wanted attention or because I thought my story was special—but because if even one person hears and understands this and decides to find Jesus so they too would recognize and take advantage of that second chance, it will be worth whatever cost I have to pay.

That is when I realized—this was not about me having answers. This was about sharing what I had witnessed.

It is not easy to share a story like this due to it being such a rare encounter. I had already shared most of the details with Jeanine and Sonja, but the memories were always on my mind. When I was around friends and church members, I found myself talking about it—sharing parts of my story with whoever was nearby.

Most people were shocked at first, then they would start asking questions. Others just sat in silence, taking it in.

One friend asked me if it hurt to die. I told her no—the moment my neck broke, I just sighed and gave up. There was no pain in death itself. It was what came after that was terrifying.

Another friend wanted to know what Jesus looked like. I described His face—kind, compassionate, somehow both powerful and gentle at the same time. "It's the same face I saw in 1994 when I first accepted Jesus," I told her. I did not know then that I was remembering Him, not just seeing a vision. My spirit recognized Him even when my mind did not.

Each conversation was different, but they all had one thing in common—people wanted to understand what happens after we die. Some told me about videos they had watched of other people who had "near-death" experiences, so I started watching a few of these videos myself.

Watching those videos was both validating and isolating. Validating because I was not alone—others had experienced the supernatural and come back to talk about it. But also isolating because so many stories were about heaven, light, peace, and love. Beautiful experiences that left people transformed and comforted.

My experience was different. I had been to the other place. The place people do not want to think about. The place people do not want to believe exists. The place people do not want to acknowledge as being real.

I watched one video where a man explained why there are so many books about what he called "positive near-death experiences" versus negative ones. The key takeaway for me was when he stated that most, if not all, negative experiences were forgotten by the person who had them—so there were not many stories available. If the person did not forget, they were often so traumatized they did not want to talk about it.

The man's explanation, about why negative experiences are rarely shared, hit me hard. I could relate to this explanation. I had not wanted to talk about it immediately after the crash, and then the amnesia set in just a few days later. Even now that I am beginning to remember, part of me wants to forget that it ever happened. Talking about it means reliving it, over and over.

You may still be wondering why I am telling this story. It is not to create some spectacle. This is not entertainment. This is about Jesus being real. The stakes could not be higher or more eternal. Second chances are rare and God's redemptive power is real. The simple truth is I want others to find Jesus. I do not want anyone to go where I went.

The decision to write this book was not easy. I kept going back and forth, unsure if I should actually do it. Then at a tea party for a local church's women's group, something happened that removed all doubt. A woman I had met a few times but did not know well, suddenly stood up and walked over to me. She had this look on her face—focused, certain, like she had something urgent to say.

"I need to tell you something," she said. "I do not usually do this, and I hope this does not seem strange, but I feel very strongly that God wants me to speak something over you."

She told me I was going to write books. She had no idea I had been wrestling with that very decision. The confirmation was clear. That was when I knew for certain that I needed to write this story and publish it as a book.

The purpose became crystal clear even though the reasons did not. I still do not know why God chose me for this experience. Why me and not someone else? Why did I have to be twelve years old? Why did the amnesia have to last 37 years—three decades of following Jesus without knowing He had already rescued me once?

I do not have those answers. Maybe I never will. Maybe understanding the 'why' is not the point. Maybe the point is simply to be faithful with what I do know— that Jesus is real, that He is faithful, that eternity is real, and that people need to find Him before it is too late.

Chapter Twenty:

The Gift of Memory

For most of my life, I have lived with significant memory loss. The crash did not just take my memories of that night—it damaged my ability to form and keep new memories. I also lost all my memories from before the crash. People do not understand what that is like unless they have experienced it, and most people do not know how to respond when they realize you cannot remember things, they think you should remember.

I would be at a family gathering and someone would say, 'Remember when we went to the lake that summer?' Everyone would laugh, sharing the memory. I would smile and nod, pretending to remember, because admitting I had no idea what they were talking about made everything awkward.

Or worse, someone would reference an important conversation we had—something I had apparently said or promised—and I would have absolutely no memory of it. 'But we talked about this last week,' they would say, frustrated. I could not explain that last week might as well have been last year for all I could recall of it.

Work was challenging too. I would have to write everything down immediately or it would vanish. Co-workers would mention projects we had discussed, and I would scramble to piece together what they were talking about without revealing I had completely forgotten. I got really good at hiding that I could not remember, so good at it that no one ever knew I had amnesia.

A friend later told me that I had been suffering in silence all those years. She was right. I never talked about my struggles with memory loss. I never asked for help or accommodations. I just pretended everything was fine and worked twice as hard to hide my limitations. Many people with invisible disabilities do this—we suffer in silence rather than burden others or risk being seen as less capable. Silence does not protect us; it just isolates us further.

You might be wondering what it is like to live with memory issues. There is a constant confusion that shadows everything. In conversations where you should know what everyone is talking about, you find yourself asking more questions than contributing knowledge. I often hear myself asking the same thing: When? When did that happen? When did we go there? In my mind I would ask myself, why don't I remember it?

Many times, I found myself drifting away from conversations just to avoid the frustration. The amnesia took an emotional toll on me—feelings of anxiety about forgetting important things, isolation from not being able to participate fully in shared memories, especially about the crash. Everyone else in the car could talk about how they felt and what they saw, but I was just clueless. I felt grief over lost experiences and moments. I felt isolated and alone.

The isolation was profound. I would be in a room full of people I knew, sharing memories I should have been part of, and feel completely alone. They were bonded by shared experiences I could not access. They had inside jokes I did not understand. They had history together that included me—but I was not really there, because I could not remember being there.

Friendships suffered. How do you maintain relationships when you are not able to remember the things that built them? When you are not able to recall conversations you had, promises you made, experiences you shared? People would reference 'that time we…' and I would have nothing. Eventually, some people stopped trying. I learned what helps by living through what doesn't.

For people with amnesia or other memory issues, please remember to be patient. It is not a choice—people do not choose to forget. Brain injuries are invisible. Just because someone looks fine does not mean they are fine. Memory loss is frustrating for the person experiencing it too, perhaps even more so. Sometimes, it is just too difficult to think.

You can help rather than add to the frustration. Here are some specific ways you can help someone with memory issues:

When they forget something, you just told them, say 'I will remind you again' instead of 'I already told you that.' The difference in tone makes all the difference in how the person receives it.

Try repeating information without showing annoyance—the person struggling will take it negatively if you show your frustration. Be patient when asked the same question multiple times. Do not make someone feel bad for forgetting. Understand that memory loss affects identity and relationships, completely.

If they are not able to remember an event they attended, do not quiz them on it. Instead, share what happened as if you are telling a story: 'At your birthday party last month, Sarah brought that chocolate cake you loved.' This gives them the information without making them feel tested.

Create memory support by taking photos to help build visual memories, or share stories to fill in gaps. For people with memory loss, pictures become their memory. I have photos of events I attended but do not remember. Those photos prove I was there, even if my brain does not access the experience.

Write things down. Not just for them, but for you too. If you had an important conversation, send a follow-up text or email summarizing what was discussed. This creates a record they can reference.

Most importantly, believe them when they say they do not remember. They are not lying or being difficult. Their brain literally does not have access to that information, no matter how important or recent it is.

Be a witness to someone's life when they do not remember it themselves and offer gentle reminders instead of criticism.

The frustrating thing for me is that I had someone who could have answered so many questions about the crash and what happened after the crash—my mother. She witnessed everything: my childhood, the crash, the aftermath. She passed away from cancer in 2012, before these specific memories returned. The loss of her was devastating on its own, but when the memories came back in 2024, I experienced a second wave of grief—grief for all the conversations about what I was beginning to remember, conversations that we could have had but never would.

There are so many questions I will never get to ask. What were the details of the crash? What changed about my behavior afterward that made our friendships end? Whose decision was it to check me out of the hospital that night? And why wouldn't she call 911 that Sunday when my head was hurting so badly? What was her perspective on my memory loss?

The grief lies in the timing—my memories returned twelve years too late. We had all that time from 1994 to 2012 when I received Jesus and was born again, becoming a follower of Jesus, when we were going to church together, when we could have talked about spiritual things. If the memories had come back then, we could have processed it together. I could have gotten her confirmation of details only she knew, like names I still cannot recall. We could have had conversations I had longed for, like finally being able to explain the broken neck.

Instead, she died still thinking I had simply survived a bad car crash. She never knew the full story. She never knew her daughter had been to hell and back.

Though perhaps it is for the best. If she had known that the boss creature wanted her instead of me, it might have terrified her.

What did the return of my memories give me? More than I could have imagined.

Understanding of my own life, finally. Why I had been so emotionally flat for years. Why I could not form deep connections. Why faith felt new in 1994 even though I had met Jesus several years earlier. It all made sense once I remembered.

Answers to lifelong questions about what happened in the crash. Connection to my past, even with gaps remaining. A sense of purpose in sharing what I remember. Validation that the unexplainable events were real. The healed neck was not a medical mystery—it was a miracle performed by the two glowing lightbulb people in the back of that crashed car. The emotional changes were not just trauma—they were the result of experiencing something beyond human comprehension. As a twelve-year-old, could I have mentally survived the memories of being inside Hell, let alone being dead?

Today I still live with incomplete memory. I have accepted that some gaps might never be filled, and that is okay. I do not need a complete memory to fulfill my purpose. I do not need every detail to share what matters. I value what I do remember rather than grieving what has been lost. I have found a place of peace with the unanswered questions. Some things I will understand in heaven. Some things do not need to be understood at all.

Living with memory loss taught me compassion—for myself and others who struggle to remember. Losing my mother before memories returned taught me that timing matters. Some questions never get answered. Some conversations never happen but the gift of memory, even when it comes late and incomplete, is still a gift.

I remember what matters most: Jesus is real, hell is real, and rescue is available right now so you never have to enter into such horror. The rest—the details my mother could have filled in—would have been nice to know, but they are not necessary to fulfill my purpose.

Chapter Twenty-One

The Missing Witness

Every supernatural event needs witnesses. I witnessed Hell, Fernando, and Jesus's rescue, but there is another witness to a different part of my story—Jill. She saw me dead. She checked my heartbeat—nothing. She checked my breathing—nothing. My body was completely lifeless in the wreckage. She looked up and saw my spirit standing outside the car in the darkness in the middle of the road, glowing like a ghost but somehow solid. She saw and talked to me through the car window while my body lay lifeless inside that upside down car.

She saw me move without walking—one moment I was standing away from the car, the next moment I was right at the window. She saw and heard me respond to her questions. She urged me to get back into my body and witnessed me fail. She witnessed the moment I vanished completely, disappearing from her sight even though she was staring right at where I had been standing.

Then, impossibly, she saw me just after I had come back to life. Hours later at the hospital, the girl who had been dead was breathing, talking, alive. No medical explanation. No logical reason. Just a miracle she witnessed but could not explain. Her testimony confirms mine.

Unfortunately, I have lost contact with her, and I do not know if she will ever know that I finally remember.

Imagine being twelve years old and watching your best friend die, then seeing her ghost standing outside the car. Imagine talking to that ghost, asking if she is dead, watching her move by thought alone. Then, imagine carrying that impossible truth your whole life while your friend has no memory of it. That was Jill's burden.

What does that do to a person? To carry impossible knowledge alone? To be called a liar or crazy when you are telling the absolute truth? To watch your best friend, forget the most significant moment you shared together?

Jill carried this burden with remarkable strength. She never recanted her story. She never said 'I was wrong' just to make people comfortable. She held onto the truth even when it cost her credibility, even when it cost her our friendship. That takes courage I can only now fully appreciate.

Looking back now with my memories restored, I wonder if things would have been different without the amnesia. Would I have told Jill what really happened? Maybe that night at the hospital, or sometime after when I was not so traumatized. Would I have told her about hell, about Fernando, about Jesus? It is hard to say what we would do differently if the outcome of a situation was different, but we can imagine.

I imagine I might have shared the truth with her eventually. She was my best friend. Maybe not right away—the experience was too raw, too terrifying. Eventually, maybe weeks or months later, I would have told her: 'You were right. I did die and I went somewhere, Jill. Somewhere terrible. But Jesus brought me back.'

We could have processed it together. She could have told me what she saw from outside my body, and I could have told her what I experienced while I was gone. We would have been the only two people who knew the complete story—her witness from the outside, my experience from the inside.

I probably would have asked her to keep it secret. At twelve years old, how do you tell people you went to hell and came back? Who would believe us? At least she would have known she was not alone in what she witnessed.

One thing I know for certain: if it had not been for the amnesia and the brain injury that stole my emotions, I never would have ended our friendship. The day when Jill and her mom were fighting was too much for my overwhelmed emotions. The sadness of it all is that it resulted in our moms fighting too. Perhaps there would have been a reconciliation if it had just been Jill and me parting ways, without our mothers getting involved.

Chapter Twenty-Two:

Letter for Jill

The cruelty of the amnesia is that it even stole my attempt to make things right with my friend Jill. For years, I did not even remember we had a fight. I did not remember losing my best friend. I went back to apologize, to fix our friendship, but no one was home. Then the amnesia took even that memory, and we never reconnected.

Once the memories came back and I knew Jill had been telling the truth all along, finding her became urgent. She deserved to know. She had carried this burden alone for 37 years. She needed to hear that she was right, that I remembered now, that she was not crazy.

Modern technology got me thinking, certainly I could find Jill. I started with internet white pages, finding several phone numbers that could be hers. Each time I dialed one of those numbers my heart raced, but the numbers led nowhere—wrong people, disconnected lines, dead ends.

Then, I found a Facebook page with her photo. It was definitely her—older, but I recognized her immediately. The page was dormant, last updated years ago. I sent a message anyway, hoping she might check it someday. No response.

Jill's mother had a Facebook page and I thought I could ask her about getting in touch with Jill, but her mom appeared to ignore my request. Perhaps she does not want Jill to start talking about seeing me as a ghost again. Maybe she is protecting her daughter from revisiting that trauma.

Maybe someday Jill will read this book. That is my hope. If I cannot reconcile in person perhaps this letter to Jill will make its way to her.

"*Dear Jill,*

So many years have passed but maybe you still remember what happened that night of the crash December 18th, 1987, when you saw me as a ghost. You were right, I had died. Everything you saw that night was real.

I understand now what it must have been like for you—to see something impossible and have no one believe you. To know the truth and be called a liar. To carry that knowledge alone for so long. I am sorry I could not remember and confirm your story and that you had to fight that battle by yourself.

What you saw was real. Every word you spoke about that night was true. You checked my heartbeat and there was not one. You saw me outside the car as a ghost just as you told everyone. We talked through the window. You watched me try to get back in my body and fail. Then you watched me come back to life anyway.

You were the only witness to my death and resurrection. Your testimony matters. It validates what I experienced and I validate what you witnessed. Together, our stories prove that the supernatural events of that night are real.

You always stayed true to what you believed. You were not traumatized or confused—you were a witness to something supernatural.

I would have liked to tell you directly rather than have you read it in a book. I finally got my memories back. You and I are the only ones that know what happened. We both experienced a supernatural event. We are not crazy, this really all happened. Hopefully reading this will help you get closure.

I do not know if we will ever reunite. I hope we see each other again in this life, but I need to be realistic. If I never see you, I want to say thank you for being a supportive friend. I hope you know how much your friendship meant to me."

Somewhere, Jill is living her life, maybe still carrying the memory of that impossible night. Maybe she has told the story so many times people do not believe her anymore. Maybe she has stopped telling it altogether. I hope someday she will read this book and know she was not alone in what she witnessed.

Thank you, Jill, for never giving up on the truth.

Living Fully in My Second Chance

I was given something most people do not get—a second chance at life. What do you do with a second chance? Not a small second chance, like getting another try at something you messed up. A real second chance— brought back from literal death, rescued from actual hell, given decades more to live.

Every morning when I wake up, I know something most people do not think about: I was not supposed to be here. By every natural law, I should have stayed dead but Jesus brought me back and I have a life to live—a life with purpose. Every breath is borrowed time. Every conversation is an opportunity. Every relationship is a gift I almost did not get to experience.

I do not take ordinary moments for granted anymore. Morning coffee. Conversations with friends. Watching a sunset. These are not just nice moments—they are bonus moments. Moments I would not have had if Jesus had not rescued me. Now I have a responsibility to honor that gift every single day.

Knowing I could have spent eternity in hell makes me realize the value in the second chance I have been given. I find myself bolder now, more willing to share my story and tell people that Jesus is the way, the truth, and the life.

When I read the Bible these days, it means more to me than it ever did. The words have not changed—they are exactly the same as they always were—but I am different. I connect the dots in ways I never could before.

For example, John 8:32: "You will know the truth, and the truth will set you free." Knowing the truth about what happened to me—about where I went and who rescued me—has set me free in ways I never imagined.

Also, in Matthew 10:28: "Do not be afraid of those who kill the body but cannot kill the soul. Rather, be afraid of the One who can destroy both soul and body in hell." I used to read that verse and think it was harsh. Now I understand it is a warning born from love. Jesus was trying to tell people the truth about what is at stake. He was warning them about the place I actually went to and that He is the only one who can make a difference.

That leads me to John 14:6: "I am the way and the truth and the life. No one comes to the Father except through me." I used to hear people say this was narrow-minded. Now I know it is just true. Jesus literally came to hell to rescue me. He is the only one who could.

The most important things in life are relationships: our relationship with God and our relationships with other people. This life is so short—we do not have time to waste on trivial things. Every person could die tomorrow and face eternity. I have seen where some of them might end up. I have witnessed the reality they do not believe in which pushes me to tell people the truth.

Some days the weight of this knowledge feels heavy—knowing the truth and watching people live like they have all the time in the world. Jesus did not rescue me from hell just so I could keep quiet about it. I have to tell people. Not in an obnoxious way—I am not standing on street corners yelling at strangers. When opportunities come, when conversations open up, when someone asks about my story, I have to be faithful to tell the truth.

I cannot save anyone—only Jesus can do that. My job is to tell what I witnessed. Some people will believe me, some will not. Some will be transformed by the story; others might dismiss it.

I wrote this book so the testimony could reach beyond my personal conversations. This is how I honor the second chance Jesus gave me—by being faithful with what He showed me. If one person chooses Jesus because they read this book, if one soul avoids hell because of what I shared, then every awkward conversation and every skeptical look is worth it. I did not ask for this experience, but I am not going to waste it. Jesus rescued me from hell. The least I can do is tell people He is real.

This book ends here, but my story continues. I am still living my second chance, still learning what it means to honor the gift Jesus gave me. Every day I wake up is another day I was not supposed to have. Every person I meet is someone I can share Jesus with – someone I might never have encountered without this second chance. Every moment matters because I know how quickly it can all end.

If you have read this book and you do not know Jesus, I am asking you: do not wait. Do not assume you have time. Do not think you will deal with it later. I was twelve years old when I died. Twelve. I thought I had my whole life ahead of me. I did not.

You could die today. Tonight. This hour. And where you go is decided by what you do right now, in this life, while you still have breath in your lungs.

Saying a prayer is not enough—I know this personally. When I was six, my mom asked me to pray a prayer to accept Jesus, and I did say the prayer. It was just words. I did not understand what I was doing. I did not truly believe. When I died at twelve, I went to hell anyway.

What saves you is not repeating words. It is truly believing in your heart that Jesus is Lord, that He died for your sins and rose again, and genuinely surrendering your life to Him. Romans 10:9 says, "If you declare with your mouth, "Jesus is Lord," and believe in your heart that God raised him from the dead, you will be saved."

It is the belief in your heart that matters. If you truly believe Jesus is who He says He is, if you genuinely want to be rescued from going to Hell, surrender to Him today. Tell Him you believe. Ask Him to save you. It does not have to be fancy words; it just has to be real and come from your heart.

Thank you for reading my story. I hope it changes how you see life, death, and eternity. Jesus will rescue anyone who calls on Him. Do not wait until you are dead to find out He is real. Choose Him now. Live your life with purpose. Make your days count and when your time comes—as it will for all of us—you will know exactly where you are going. That is my prayer for you. That is how I am choosing to live fully in my second chance.